THE LAW SCHOOL HUSTLE

How to Get the Grades, Get the Job, and Get the Checks!

Ashley N. Kirkwood, Esq.

November Media Publishing, Chicago IL.

Copyright © 2018 Ashley N. Kirkwood, Esq.

All rights reserved. No part of this publication may be reproduced, distributed, or transmitted in any form or by any means, including photocopying, recording, or other electronic or mechanical methods, without the prior written permission of the publisher, except in the case of brief quotations embodied in critical reviews and certain other noncommercial uses permitted by copyright law. For permission requests, write to the publisher, addressed "Attention: Permissions Coordinator," at the email address below.

November Media Publishing info@novembermediapublishing.com

Ordering Information: Special discounts are available on quantity purchases by corporations, associations, and others. For details, contact the publisher at the email address above.

Printed in the United States of America

Produced & Published by November Media Publishing

ISBN: 978-1-7326897-0-1

First Edition : September 2018

10 9 8 7 6 5 4 3 2 1

TABLE OF CONTENTS

FOREWORD ix

Chapter I. My Personal Law School Hustle 1

**Chapter II To Master The Game, You Must Learn
    The Rules** 9

    A. Evaluate Each School That Accepts You—Look
    at the Numbers 12

    B. Should You Work While in Law School? 13

Chapter III. Create Your Game Plan Before Day One 19

    A. Helpful Things to Purchase 20

    B. Speak with Successful Students 20

    C. Maintaining Relationships and Your Sanity 22

**Chapter IV. MONEY, MONEY, MONEY: loans
    VS. scholarships** 25

CHAPTER V. **Crush Your G.p.a. Goals** 31

    A. Preparing for Class: IRAC 32

        1. Facts 33

    2. Issue 34
    3. Rule 35
    4. Application 36
    5. Conclusion 37
  B. Attending Class 38

    1. Office Hours 39
  C. Practice Examinations 41

  D. Spotting the Issues 44

  E. Learn the Law: The Importance of Rote Memorization 46

    1. Flashcards 46
      a. Creating Your Own Flashcards *46*

      b. Commercial Flashcards *49*

      c. Writing the Law *50*

      d. Listening to the Law *50*

  F. Study Groups: It Depends—Who Do You Trust? 51

Chapter VI. It will take more than good grades 57

  A. Character and Fitness 57

  B. Networking 59

    1. Bar Associations 60
    2. Alumni 63

Chapter VII. Land The Job You Want 73

  A. Summer Associate Positions 73

  B. Internships 77

  C. Externships 78

  D. Law Clerks 79

E. Fellowships 80

F. Develop a Career Action Plan 80

G. Getting Interviews 83

H. Interviewing...84

Chapter VIII. 2L Year Focuses On Employment: Stay Hungry 87

A. On-Campus Interviewing (OCI) 87

   1. But My School Doesn't Have OCI! 89
   2. Additional Interviewing Tips..89
   3. Dress to Impress 94

B. 2L2: Looking Toward the Summer..94

C. I Still Don't Have A Job 95

D. Extra-Curricular Activities..97

CHAPTER IX. It's not over till' it's over: 3l year 99

   1. Confirm Your Graduation Requirements..........................100
   2. Fulfill the Requirements to Practice Law..........................101
      a. Prepare for the Bar Examination *102*

Chapter X. You Control Your Destiny: Transferring Law Schools...109

A. How to Transfer..110

B. Was It Worth It? 112

Appendix A Helpful Law School Supplements 115

I would like to dedicate this book to my loving husband, Christopher Kirkwood, who supports me in every endeavor, big or small; my parents, Keith and Valerie Williams, and my brother, Wilbert Williams, as they have always given me lofty goals to pursue as well as the confidence to achieve them. Lastly, I would like to thank my aunt and uncle Steffany and Jason Cunningham, who helped inspire me to go to law school.

FOREWORD

So you've decided to go to law school, huh? Unquestionably you have heard countless horror stories about the lack of jobs, the high cost of law school tuition, and the difficulties of succeeding once admitted. Despite all that, you are here, reading this book, and guess what? You have taken a step in the right direction. Good lawyers do their research, and that is what you are doing by reading this book—researching strategies for law school success. Before diving into strategies that you can use to dominate law school, I want to tell you a little about myself.

I am a trial attorney in Chicago, Illinois, a former career advisor, and a not-so-great student turned scholar. By reading this book, you will learn the strategies I used to excel on law school examinations, ace legal interviews, obtain law school scholarships and transfer from a fourth-tier law school to one of the highest-ranked law schools in the country. This is an easy to follow guidethat seeks to arm you with the tools needed to successfully navigate your new legal career. Now, you will notice that this book has footnotes. The footnotes in this book provide you with additional details about the legal profession. You should feel free to reference them, as they are packed with gems to help you navigate your law school journey.

I have seen the strategies in this book enhance the performance of countless students that I have coached throughout their law school careers. I believe in the benefits of a legal education, whether you decide to practice or not, and thus you will not hear much gloom and doom from me about law school or the legal profession. I enjoyed law school, and with a little strategy, the legal profession can still provide ample opportunities for success. You can do this, you will do this, and this book will help.

*"Hustle beats talent when talent
doesn't hustle"*
—Unknown

CHAPTER I.

MY PERSONAL LAW SCHOOL HUSTLE

WARNING!! This is the section of the book where I talk about myself. I know, I know, you want me to get straight to the part where I give you the keys to law school success, but I promise I have a (somewhat) interesting story. If you really cannot take it and you are comfortable blindly taking my advice, so be it—you can skip this section. But if you need some convincing, read on.

I was born in January 1990 to two loving parents . . . Wait—let me skip to the part that is directly applicable to this book's topic. I went to the University of Illinois at Urbana-Champaign (UIUC) and majored in international business. Despite my *less than best* efforts, I graduated—barely—with a 2.1 GPA. You are probably thinking, "Crap, why the heck did I buy a book from a girl who had a 2.1 GPA?! I'm doomed." But keep reading, it gets better. Despite my abysmal undergraduate academic performance, I graduated from Northwestern University Pritzker School of Law (Northwestern) with a 3.86 GPA and upon graduation accepted a position with one of Chicago's top litigation firms [insert sigh of relief here.] But how? Well, I am not a naturally gifted test taker, but I am an unbelievably (some would say) hard worker and a master strategist. I often say, when speaking to students, that everything I did to achieve success in law school, both academically and professionally, can be taught, memorized, and implemented by others—and that is the good news!

Another point of order: you are probably wondering how, with a 2.1 GPA, I received admittance into Northwestern in the first place. Well, the long and short of it is this: at first, I didn't. In fact, when I initially applied to law school, I didn't get into any law school—not even one. But I didn't give up, in part because I have always known I wanted to practice law. One thing my father taught me is that when someone gives you a "no," they just aren't the right person to give you the "yes" you need. Don't give up—strategize.

I applied to law school three times in total: the first time, not a single school accepted me; the second time, The John Marshall Law School (John Marshall) granted me conditional acceptance (more on this later); and the third time, Northwestern accepted me as a transfer student.

John Marshall was the first law school to accept me. John Marshall essentially looked past my undergraduate performance and saw that I could be a successful law student and eventually a successful lawyer. Earlier I noted that I was granted conditional acceptance. Conditional acceptance programs permit students to attend classes the summer before the fall semester begins to prove that they can handle the academic rigors of law school. John Marshall's conditional acceptance program permitted me to attend summer classes and, if I received a 2.5 GPA or higher, I would gain full admittance into the law school. You may be thinking, "A 2.5 GPA?! How hard can that be?" Good question. Well, I'll put it like this: out of the students admitted to this program, only around 50 percent received full admittance into the law school. Even with a full-time job, I completed the program (which consisted of three evening classes) and loved every minute of it. When grades came out, I learned that I received the highest GPA in the program, and as a result of my success, I was awarded a small scholarship to help with my first-year (1L) expenses.[1] This was the start to a great academic journey. During my first year of law school, I worked hard and enjoyed classes; I earned all A's and obtained a 1L summer associate position with one of the nation's largest management-side

---

[1] You will often see me use terms such as "1L," "2L" and "3L"; these simply designate a law student's year in school. For instance, a first-year law student is a "1L," a second-year law student is a "2L", etc.

employment law firms.[2] All in all, it was a good year.[3]

When John Marshall accepted me, I felt nothing but pure excitement. Yet soon after I started law school, elitism—a staple of the legal profession—began to rear its ugly head. When I met attorneys and proudly told them where I attended school, some would congratulate me, but many warned of the difficulty I would face when seeking postgraduate employment because I attended a fourth-tier law school.[4] This devastated me, but I didn't have much

---

[2] Management-side employment law firms represent employers, whereas plaintiff-side employment law firms represent employees.

[3] 1L Summer Associate positions are typically paid summer positions at medium to large law firms, where you can make anywhere from $2,000 to $3,500 a week. Because of the high pay, great experience, and possibility that the summer position might convert into full-time employment upon graduation, these positions are coveted and hard to obtain. Typically, students interested in the private sector seek these opportunities.

[4] There is some debate surrounding this topic, but as used in this book, law schools ranked from 1–50 are considered "tier one"; schools ranked 51–100 are considered "tier two"; schools ranked 101–150 are considered "tier three" and schools ranked 151–200 are considered "tier four." In 1987, *U.S. News* disrupted (some would argue) the legal market by creating its "Best Law School Rankings," which ranked schools in numerical order, with the fourteen top-ranked schools in the nation being colloquially referenced as the "T-14." *See generally* Christopher J. Ryan, Jr. & Brian L. Frye, A Revealed-Preferences Ranking of Law Schools, 69 ALA. L.R. 495, 497 (2017).

time to wallow. I needed a strategy. After speaking with several mentors, I decided I wanted to start my career at a large law firm. After researching the number of law school graduates from fourth-tier schools that land jobs at large firms, I decided to transfer to a more highly ranked law school. I set my sights on Northwestern. I then drafted a strong transfer application, interviewed with an admission counselor, and received admittance into Northwestern as a transfer law student.

I graduated *cum laude* (GPA 3.86) from Northwestern and, after passing the Illinois bar examination, I started as an associate at Kirkland & Ellis LLP, one of the nation's largest and most prestigious law firms. Throughout my six semesters of law school, I received two B+'s (I'm still slightly salty about that one semester ruining my straight-A streak, but as Mama would say, I turned out all right) but the rest of my grades were A's, A–'s, or A+'s. In light of this book's topics, I think that is important to note.[5] In addition to getting good grades in law school, I developed strong ties to the legal community and re-

---

5   I advise seeking academic mentors—individuals at your school who have taken your courses and have performed well. To find the right academic mentors, you will need to find out whether they performed well academically. One easy way to do this is to ask a counselor, or professor, if there is someone who has performed well that they recommend you speak with about how to excel academically. It is likely that they will point you to the academic rock stars you seek.

ceived over $50,000 in outside scholarships (notable because many T-14[6] schools do not award transfer students scholarships).

I present a bit about my background so that you can take my advice in context. I will not have the answers for every law student. In fact, I share my career goals because, depending on what you want out of your legal career, the path that I traveled may not be the ideal path for you. I loved law school but not everyone will. Illustrative of this, many who love being lawyers often recount law school as a horrible and distant memory.

I worked before law school. I like working. I worked during law school, at least part-time, almost every semester. That may or may not be for you. I met and married my husband before law school. That also shaped the way I approached school. Law school was really important to me, but my focus was divided between being a good law student, building a strong professional reputation, andlaying the foundation for a strong marriage. To accomplish this, I tried (albeit sometimes unsuccessfully) to have a date night every week during law school. My values were God, family, and then school, in that order. Your values will affect how you approach law school, and that's a good

---

6   "T-14" is shorthand for one of the top fourteen law schools in the nation. For example, Northwestern, in 2017, was ranked by *U.S. News and World Report* as being the number-ten law school in the country. Therefore, Northwestern is a T-14 school.

thing. Things will shift, and you will bend, as will those who love and support you, but your life will not stop for law school. A great friend of mine once said, "Work stops for life; life doesn't stop for work." That same thinking applies to school. Law school takes a lot of time, but it should not consume your entire life. My genuine desire is for every law student to achieve success while still living his or her bestlife. Everyone has different metrics and indicators for success, but if your goal is to achieve great grades as a part of that success, this book is for you. Law school is a personal journey, but in my experience, it is hard to travel anywhere, regardless of the destination, without a map. Let this book be your map.

*"You have to learn the rules of the game and then
you have to play better than anyone else."*
—Albert Einstein

CHAPTER II

TO MASTER THE GAME, YOU MUST LEARN THE RULES

How should you select which law school to attend? Well, how many options do you have and what are your options? As a general rule, you should go to the highest-ranked law school you can afford. In some instances, I even suggest taking out debt to attend a higher-ranked law school, but first you have to ask yourself some questions. As an initial step, think about how you want to use your law degree.

If you are 100 percent positive you want to dedicate your life to public service, it may not be wise to take on hundreds of thousands of dollars of debt to attend a highly-ranked law school when you can attend a reasonably-ranked school for free. On the other hand, if you know you want to work at a large law firm, then you will find that the ranking of your law school matters quite a bit. One article notes that school "prestige" is the number one factor that elite employers consider when deciding where they will focus their recruitment efforts.[7] Moreover, out of the 37,124 law students that graduated in 2016, only 16 percent made the BigLaw[8] starting salary of $180,000.[9]

The truth is, your job prospects and probability of academic success skyrocket with the ranking of the school. To explain further, the higher the school's ranking, in many instances, the more forgiving the grading curve. I know this from personal experience. At my first law school, it was not uncommon for a certain percentage of students to receive D's and *even F's*, but at Northwestern, that was a lot less common. At Northwestern, professors were not mandated to give students failing grades, and in fact it was rare that a student received such grades. Is that fair? Maybe not. Nonetheless, many, but not all, higher-ranked schools employ grading curves that are **more**

---

[7] Elite services firms, including law firms, use prestige as the primary factor when considering from which schools to recruit. Lauren Rivera, *Firms Are Wasting Millions Recruiting On Only A Few Campuses*, Harvard Business Review (Oct. 23, 2015).

[8] "BigLaw" is just a colloquial nickname for the largest law firms in the nation. Most of these firms pay the "market" starting salary to new associate attorneys, which, when I started was $160,000. That salary has now increased.

[9] Stacy Zaretsky, Sorry, Law Students, But Your Starting Salary Will Not Be $190K, Above The Law (Jun 7, 2018); *see also* ALA Section of Legal Education and Admissions to the Bar, Employment Outcomes As of April 2018 (Class of 2017 Graduates).

forgiving than those at lower-ranked schools. Some law schools even dismiss students after the first semester. All this to say, if you are unsure about what you want to do with your career, that's okay, but you want to put yourself in the strongest position to succeed no matter the career field you choose to enter.

Next, consider whether you are willing to wait to attend law school. If only one law school accepts you, you have to decide whether you will attend the one school that accepted you or whether you will apply again after making yourself a more competitive applicant. I faced this choice. I received admittance into one school. For me, the choice was simple—I wasn't waiting anymore. I was ready to go to law school. So I went, saddled up with debt from the federal government, and began my law school journey. By this time, I had taken the Law School Admissions Test (LSAT) twice, and although my score increased the second time, it wasn't good enough to convince a T-14 school to admit me.[10] Still, I knew that if I could just get into law school, I could excel. If you know that you can wait, spend more time studying, and get a higher LSAT score, it may be worth it to do so. Take the LSAT again, increase your score, and in turn increase your chances of attending a tier-one law school the first time around.

---

10   The LSAT is the entrance exam that almost every American Bar Association (ABA)-approved law school requires to evaluate whether or not a student will receive acceptance.

A. Evaluate Each School That Accepts You— Look at the Numbers

Most prospective law students will have more options than I had. Take your time and make the right choice. Visit each school. Sit in on a few classes if you have the time. Also, check the numbers. Look up the school's alumni employment rates. Many schools publish their graduates' employment rates after a nine-month period— meaning they make public the number of graduates that found employment nine months after graduation. But who wants to wait nine months for a job? Ask the admissions office for the rate of students with employment *at graduation*. If you are interested in the private sector, research graduates' average salary at graduation, speak with both alumni and current students, and keep track of your findings so that you can easily compare schools. Make an Excel chart and compare the data for your prospective law schools:

Law School Name	% Employed at Graduation	% of Alumni in the Private Sector	% of Alumni in the Public Sector	Average Starting Salary	Grading Curve Data

Take a lawyer with you to visit some schools (if feasible) and ask him or her to help you develop questions for the admissions officer. This is the first step of your legal career. A mantra that I heard all the time from my mentors was, "No one will care more about your career than you." Your legal career does not start with your first legal job; it starts with law school. Don't phone this one in—do the research, and choose wisely.

B. Should You Work While in Law School?

Most people will tell you not to work during law school, especially during your first year, but I won't give you such blanket advice. The reality is, some law students might need to work during law school. Working during my first year of law school helped me perform at a high level. I voluntarily worked during law school for several reasons. I worked to gain experience in the private sector of law. I attended law school to become an employment lawyer but had no employment law experience. If you want to specialize early in your career, you will have to explain how you know that you are interested in that particular field. Working helped me to demonstrate my interest in employment law.

In addition to needing experience, I also wanted to generate income and expand my perspective. I attended school during the day and worked part-time after class. To be candid, however, my primary financial support during law school came from my husband, so I was fortunate to be able to work a flexible job to supplement our household income. During my first semester of law school, I worked part-time for a brilliant attorney, Fern Trevino, at

The Law Offices of Fern Trevino. She was extremely flexible when it came to scheduling my hours.

How did I find this job, you ask? I Googled "plaintiff-side employment law firms in Chicago," called the first firm on the list, and told them that I'd recently begun law school and wanted to work part-time at an employment law firm. By God's grace, the first firm that answered my call happened to be hiring, brought me in for an interview, and offered me a position the same day. I started working a few days after my interview. Working for a plaintiff's lawyer made me more attractive to defense employment firms, and eventually I was able to land a lucrative summer position with a large management-side employment law firm. Every decision in law school should involve some level of strategy. You have limited time as a law student, so you need to ask yourself, will this opportunity/class/school/networking event/etc. help me reach my end goal? If the answer is "yes" and it does not conflict with your values or course load, then go for it!

To answer the question of whether *you* should work, you must determine whether, first and foremost, you need to work to survive. If you do, then work—end of analysis. If you don't need to work to survive, then working should be a strategic decision. Do you want to practice law in a particular field in which you have no experience? If the answer is "yes," then working or volunteering (which is typically more flexible) may be the right decision for you.

After determining you want to work, you have to be very strategic in selecting a job. You want a job that is flexible and provides invaluable experience. After receiving a particular job offer, you need to ask the hard questions about scheduling before accepting the offer. A great way to handle this is to propose, to the extent that you can, a schedule that accommodates your classes soon after receiving the offer. Moreover, let your employer know in advance which days you need to take off from work based on your final exam schedule. Securing vacation days before starting your new position should eliminate confusion and set you up for success. Be direct, respectful, and professional during scheduling conversations, and get everything discussed in writing or send a follow-up email memorializing your employment terms.

Though working can be a great experience, with every "yes" you are saying "no" to something else. That means you must determine what you are giving up by working. What will you do if you find yourself falling behind in your classes? Will you quit your job? Will you request additional days off from work? Will either decision negatively impact your professional brand? Additionally, can you work and still participate in extracurricular activities? Is that important to you? In summation, working may be right for you, but if you cannot work and obtain stellar grades, and you don't have to work to survive, then don't do it. This is **your** law school journey. Don't let anyone mess it up—not even you.

Once you have selected a school, be confident in your selection and in your ability to succeed in law school. You can do this. Law school attracts the best and the brightest (if I do say so myself). You will be competing with students who have excelled academically and/or professionally (in some instances) all of their lives, but you are seated right next to them. You must have confidence. Asking questions takes confidence. Admitting you don't understand a particular legal concepttakes confidence. Telling your family and friends you have new prioritiestakes confidence. You will also need confidence to draft a well-written exam under extreme time pressures. You won't have time to second-guess yourself when the clock is ticking. Convincing an employer to hire you takes confidence. I am not suggesting that you be boastful, but rather that you remain confident in your ability to excel in law school. So many of my peers continuously discussed how hard classes were and how they were sure they would fail this exam or that exam. Don't be that person. You will not fail. You will work hard and invest in your education, and you will get a good return on that investment. Only speak those things that you want to manifest in your life. Have faith that you will succeed, put in the work, and watch your hard work pay off. You know what builds confidence? Preparation. Let's discuss what you can do to prepare before your first day of law school.

"You were born to win, but to be a winner, you must plan to win, prepare to win, and expect to win."
—*Zig Ziglar*

CHAPTER III.

CREATE YOUR GAME PLAN BEFORE DAY ONE

Before starting law school, I recommend getting organized. Get a planner and map out your days. Plan every hour of the school week to optimize studying, reading for class, and relaxing (yes, you should plan your downtime). Additionally, if you are a student with a family or an ailing family member that you care for, you should schedule when you will handle those responsibilities. Likewise, read as much as you can about law school and the Socratic Method, which is the method used by many law professors to this day. Learn what IRAC means.[11] Read blogs about law school success. Walk the campus of your soon-to-be law school so that you know where to go on day one. Determine whether you can observe a summer class at your prospective school. Make a

---

11 This is discussed in chapter five of this book, but as a preview, "IRAC" is an acronym that stands for: **I**ssue, **R**ule, **A**pplication, and **C**onclusion. You will read countless cases in law school, and will need (and will be grateful for) a way to take organized notes that help you to summarize the cases and recall the laws discussed; the IRAC method of summarizing cases helps you to do just that.

calendar and include important dates. You should mark the date by which you will begin studying for finals and applying to internships.

A. Helpful Things to Purchase

I recommend you purchase the following before starting law school: (1) a book holder and (2) an additional computer screen. Both items proved invaluable to me. I carried my book holder with me everywhere. I set it up during class so that I could easily reference the page the professor was talking about while taking notes. Trust me—it's worth the ten-dollar investment!Similarly, an additional computer screen is awesome for several reasons. You will conduct a lot of legal research in law school. Most of the databases are now online. You will be able to write a lot faster if you have one screen displaying the case you are citing and another displaying your paper or brief. Furthermore, you will cite a lot of cases and secondary sources; having two screens will make referencing quotes from cases much easier. Now that I am practicing, I still use dual monitors. Therefore, this investment can pay dividends even after law school.

B. Speak with Successful Students

Before day one, ask the admissions office to connect you with a successful student who can answer school-specific questions that you may have. Upperclassmen often hold the keys to the law school kingdom. Upperclassmen can tell you which classes to take and which to avoid, provide you with outlines, give professor-specific tips, and even show you around campus. Asking upperclassmen for outlines is especially crucial. Outlines are crucial in law school because you will be reading hundreds of pages per week. Sometimes you are tested on a semester's worth of information just once at the very end of the semester, which means summarizing material in a way that can help you easily recall a large amount of information is important. Although many suggest you should make your own outlines, I think you should ask someone who performed well in your class previously (with the same professor) for their outline. If you ask for an outline at the beginning of the semester, you can take it with you to class and edit it as the course proceeds to fit your professor's style of teaching and your style of learning. This strategy should help you to see the big picture and provide you with a roadmap to use when (and if) you decide to create your own outline. Your outline may be as large as 100 pages, so starting from scratch can be daunting. Be sure to include examples of key cases in your outline and note pages from the textbook where material is covered. This will help when you go back at the end of the semester to complete your review and you need a refresher on the material – you will know where to look in your course book for help.

Yes, you are in law school and not undergrad, and yes, you are an adult now and can figure most things out, but why not get help from someone who has mastered the very campus where you now seek to succeed? Speak to students who previously took your classes. Ask them about their biggest law school regrets, and which classes they wish they had taken but didn't. You can learn so much just by talking to those around you. One thing to keep in mind: there is nothing wrong with getting advice from multiple sources, but in the end, when it comes to succeeding in law school, always, and I mean always, defer to your professor. There is the law, that's one thing, and then there is the law as told by your professor—that's the law you should use on your exams!

C. Maintaining Relationships and Your Sanity

Say it with me: don't let law school ruin your life. Again, don't let law school ruin your life. Maintaining relationships in law school requires deliberate effort, but I am of the mind that family comes first. This does not mean, however, that you can hang out with them in the same way during law school that you did before law school. You may need to plan your time more strategically as a law student.

Let me set the stage with a personal example. My husband and I married shortly before graduating college (yes, we were young lovebirds—and are now only slightly older lovebirds). That meant that when I started law school, I was about one year into my marriage, and I was determined to mirror my parents' positive example of going on date nights. Therefore, I set my study schedule around my life, and not vice versa. I had a few staples from my pre–law school life that I maintained throughout law school: (1) date nights, (2) church, and (3) Sunday dinners with family. During law school, to maintain my relationships and keep my sanity, I completed all my required reading and briefingof cases on the weekend and took practice tests during the week.[12] I maintained my Friday night date nights (for the most part), and whenever possible, my husband would help me study by drilling flashcards with me, which assisted me in memorizing rules and legal concepts. Because I attended church on Sundays, I woke up at 5 a.m. to complete my reading before church; this allowed me to spend the remainder of my Sunday with family. Balance is possible, but you must prioritize and keep a calendar.

---

12 Briefing a case involves taking notes on a case. Specifically, a "briefed" case will include (1) the legal issue discussed by the case, (2) the legal rule that resulted from the case, (3) how the court applied that rule to the facts of the particular case, and (4) the conclusion of the case. Many people also include the key facts from the case and its procedural history (i.e., how the case arrived at the appellate court, as most cases you will read in law school will be at either the federal or state appellate or supreme court level—although some exceptions may apply).

"The dream is free; the hustle is sold separately."
—*Unknown*

CHAPTER IV.

MONEY, MONEY, MONEY: LOANS VS. SCHOLARSHIPS

Law school is expensive. I took on a lot of debt to attend law school. If you get good grades in undergrad and perform well on the LSAT, it is likely that you can receive a scholarship to attend law school. Because that wasn't my situation, I didn't. So, in order to help pay for law school, I took out loans for the first year, then started speaking to upperclassmen and the financial aid office about scholarship opportunities. Most schools will have a list or a book of various outside scholarships that are available. You should go through the list carefully, identify which scholarships you plan to apply for, and then develop a calendar containing the deadlines by which to apply.

I received the vast majority of my scholarships from bar associations. I also participated in legal writing contests to win scholarship money. When looking for scholarships you should lean on your school. It is likely that the financial aid office knows where students have received money in the past. In addition, be sure to research on your own. There are some databases that specifically list scholarships. As pictured below, a quick Google search for "Law School Scholarship Databases" returns several lists compiled by scholarship websites and law schools containing numerous scholarships:

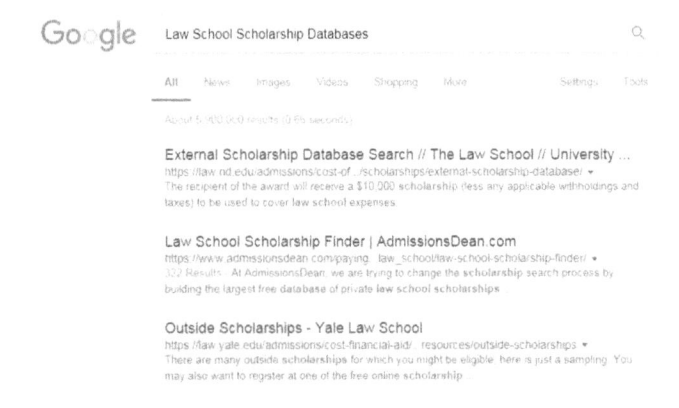

> **Google** Law School Scholarship Databases
>
> All News Images Videos Shopping More   Settings Tools
>
> About 5,900,000 results (0.65 seconds)
>
> **External Scholarship Database Search // The Law School // University ...**
> https://law.nd.edu/admissions/cost-of-.../scholarships/external-scholarship-database/ ▾
> The recipient of the award will receive a $10,000 scholarship (less any applicable withholdings and taxes) to be used to cover law school expenses.
>
> **Law School Scholarship Finder | AdmissionsDean.com**
> https://www.admissionsdean.com/paying-.../law_school/law-school-scholarship-finder/ ▾
> 322 Results. At AdmissionsDean, we are trying to change the scholarship search process by building the largest free database of private law school scholarships
>
> **Outside Scholarships - Yale Law School**
> https://law.yale.edu/admissions/cost-financial-aid/.../resources/outside-scholarships ▾
> There are many outside scholarships for which you might be eligible; here is just a sampling. You may also want to register at one of the free online scholarship ...

Many of the scholarship lists compiled by law schools do not restrict law students from other law schools from accessing the list. Those scholarship databases are gold because unlike a general scholarship database, the scholarship lists compiled by law schools have been (at least theoretically) vetted and confirmed. If you spend one hour a week researching scholarships and one hour a week compiling application materials for scholarships, you will begin to see the impact on your student loan debt. Trust me.

If you want to win outside scholarship awards, you have to tailor your application to the organization to which you are applying. You should also try to meet members of the scholarship board and ask them what they are looking for in an application. You would be surprised how willing people are to meet with you. Better yet, many scholarship organizations list the names of previous scholarship recipients on their websites. You could reach out to past winners and ask them what they did to receive the award. They may even let you read their winning essay or application.

I received scholarships from various bar associations, including the Black Women Lawyers' Association of Chicago, the Defense Research Institute, the Diversity Scholarship Foundation, the Illinois Judicial Council, and the Cook County Bar Association. First, if you fit into a minority category of any kind you should apply for scholarships set aside for your minority group. The pool of applicants will be smaller and you have a higher chance of actually receiving an award. That stated, cast a wide net. There are so many scholarships available to law students that you may want to set some parameters for yourself and goals for each month. For instance, in July, before you start law school, you can make a list of all of the upcoming scholarship deadlines for scholarships over $5,000. Be sure to list the name of the scholarship, the date the application opens, the due date, and the requirements needed to apply. Many scholarships require letters of recommendation. Be sure to give your recommenders at least one week to write your letters of recommendation.

Networking can help you to obtain outside scholarships. You should volunteer with local legal organizations that provide outside scholarships. Some scholarship applications will ask about your involvement with the respective organization issuing the scholarship. It helps if you can show that you have volunteered with the organization in the past.

Many scholarships have GPA requirements. Therefore, in addition to following directions to a tee, your strongest asset will be having outstanding grades. Let's discuss how you can get the grades that will make you competitive for scholarships and jobs!

"Hustle isn't just working on the things you like. It means doing the things you don't enjoy so you can do the things you love."
—Unknown

CHAPTER V.

CRUSH YOUR G.P.A. GOALS

You will hear this a million times, but let me be the first to tell you that grades matter—a lot. Earning a high GPA will pay dividends. Most legal employers are looking at (1) the school you attended and (2) the grades you obtained while there. If your school is not highly ranked, but you earned high grades there, you may be more marketable than someone who attended a highly-ranked school but earned a low GPA. Your primary job1L year is to obtain a stellar GPA. That's it. Do not take this to mean that you have to eat, sleep, and bathe in the library. In fact, being an effective student has very little to do with how many hours you spend in the library, but everything to do with how and what you study. Before studying, however, you need to figure out how you learn. At this point in your life, you have probably experienced some level of success in school, but law school is different. There is a heavy emphasis on writing, reading comprehension, and memorization of the law. In some instances, 100 percent of your grade in a particular course is determined by your performance on one exam—more than likely a three-to five-hour written exam. Therefore, it is important to focus on becoming not only a great writer but a persuasive one. How do you do that? Practice. One way, among many, to succeed in law school is to take practice tests early and often. However, before you begin taking practice tests you must learn how to write an exam and prepare for class, both of which will require you to understand the IRAC method of outlining your case briefs and exam answers.

A. Preparing for Class: IRAC

Before class, read all assigned reading. In law school, you will read a ton of judicial opinions, commonly referred to as "cases." Judicial opinions explain the facts of the case, the dispute between the parties, and the judge's determination as it relates to that dispute. Briefing a case is essentially outlining the case in a particular fashion. Specifically, it entails using the IRAC method to summarize the facts and law explained within a particular case. To be best prepared for class, you should briefall of the assigned cases. If you come across a case that you simply do not understand, you should Google the case and read summaries of the case that may be written in plain language. Then, after gaining a high-level understanding of what the case is about, go back and re-read the case. This should help you to pull out the important details of the case. Many of the cases you will read in law school are so important that other students and attorneys have also read and summarized those same cases. That stated, everything you read on the internet is not true, which is why it is important that if you read a summary of a particular case online you also go back, read, and brief the case yourself.

You will brief all of your cases using the IRAC method. IRAC is an acronym that stands for: Issue, Rule, Application, and Conclusion. In addition to including the issue (or the legal dispute between the parties), the resulting rule, how the court applied that rule, and the conclusion, you should also include the factual background of the case as well as the procedural posture of the case. The section of your brief containing the procedural posture will explain what happened before each court that has heard the case. For example, if you are reading a Supreme Court case, in many instances, *at least* two other courts have heard the facts of that case and made a determination. Your procedural history section, then, should include a summary of the determinations of both the district and appellate courts. Most cases are organized in IRAC format. Meaning, first the court discusses the facts of the case; within the fact section, you will often find any relevant procedural history. Next, the court addresses the legal standard by which it will adjudicate the dispute. Then, the court applies the legal standard to the facts. Lastly, the court makes its determination.

1. Facts

Include the key facts of the case in your brief. The facts section should set forth the important facts of the case.

Include the name of the case, the litigants, and key events and dates on which they occurred. For contracts cases, it is particularly important to note dates. I suggest setting up the key facts of a case in a chart. Assuming your case involved a contract dispute between Penny and Bill, you could set up your chart as follows:

Date	Event
9/1/2011	Penny made Bill an offer to purchase his car
10/1/2011	Bill accepted Penny's offer

Creating a chart is helpful because in class you will be asked questions about the case, and despite your best efforts, after reading 100+ cases in one week, it may be difficult to remember all of the factual details of a particular case.

2. Issue

What is the legal issue that the court is deciding? In a contracts case, the legal issue may be "whether Bill and Penny entered into an enforceable contract when the terms of their agreement was never memorialized?" When setting up your issue statement, you should follow this format:

Whether [Insert Legal Issue] when [Insert Key Facts].

The above-referenced format will help you craft focused issue statements. A large part of law school is learning to spot issues, which means looking at a set of facts to determine what legal concepts are in dispute. Reading cases will help you to spot legal issues. When you are reading cases for class, as you are reading the facts, you will start to identify which legal issues are present. For instance, if you read a set of facts discussing an agreement between two or more parties, you will begin to realize what types of contract-related legal issues are at play. On your law school exams, you will be given a set of facts, and the professor may ask you at the end of a long set of facts what legal issues are presented. You will then have to identify all of the legal issues presented within a particular set of facts. The more cases you read, and the more law you learn, the easier it will be to spot issues. Therefore, it is important to read all assigned cases, and identify the legal issues presented by the facts at issue.

3. Rule

The rule is the black-letter law applied to determine the outcome of the case. For example, your rule statement may be "an offer terminates when the offeree, the person receiving the offer, learns of the offeror's intent to contract with someone else." The rule is the legal standard that the case discusses. You will want to know the rules cold, but be aware that in at least some of your classes you will read older cases to see how the rules of law have changed over time. Nonetheless, paying attention to rule statements is imperative. Also, remember that you should try before class to list all applicable rule statements, but during class revise your rule statements to align with those provided by your professor. When writing your rule statements, write the page number where you found the rule statement. That way, if you are challenged in class, or have questions about the rule statement, you can easily reference the page number where you found the statement of law. This also makes it easier to ask your professor questions. For instance, you may be confused about the rule the court applied to determine the case, but it would not be prudent to ask your professor what is the applicable rule. Instead, pose the question like this: "I thought the rulewas stated on page 15, but I am not sure, can you let me know whether I am on the right track?" Professors prefer to answer questions after you have showed that you put some thought into the answer on your own.

4. Application

This section of your case brief will detail how the court appliedthe rule of law to the facts of a particular case. The application section is an essential portion of your case brief because this section shows you how the rule of law is applied to determine the case. Pay attention to how the court explains its decision, because on exams your professor will want to see that you can effectively and persuasively apply the rules of law to the facts in order to reach a conclusion. When drafting the application section, it is very important to note the significance of a particular fact.

For example, your fact section may note that:

- Before Bill could purchase Penny's car, as agreed, she instead sold it to Sam.
- Sam then told Bill he purchased the car.

Those above-referenced facts would be listed in the facts section of your case brief, but those same facts may reappear in the application section, but with a focus on *the legal significance* of those facts. Your application statement may look something like this:

- Bill's acceptance was ineffective because Bill learned of Penny's sale to Sam *before* accepting Penny's offer.

In the above example, there was legal significance to the fact that Sam told Bill that he had purchased the car from Penny before Bill accepted Penny's offer. The fact that Bill knew Penny sold the car to Sam meant that Bill could no longer accept Penny's offer to sell the car. Thus, it is important when reading a case to pay attention to the fact section, but pay even closer attention to which facts help the court reach its ultimate conclusion.

5. Conclusion

Your conclusion statement is simply the court's determination. The conclusion should answer the issue statement and make clear the action the court took to resolve the dispute. For example, if the issue presented in the case is whether Bill and Penny had a contract, the conclusion would be that the court found that Bill and Penny did not have a contract and thus the court affirmed the district court's opinion (assuming this fictitious case is on appeal). Your conclusion should include both the legal conclusion and what action the court took as a result of its conclusion.

B. Attending Class

Attend class. This one seems easy, but it's important—and don't just attend, but show up. There is a difference between attending class and showing up. Showing up involves engaging and asking questions when you have them. That last bit is vital. You need to speak up if you don't understand a particular topic. You may feel weird at first, but ask your questions anyway. Please, trust me on this. You are probably not the only one with questions. If you are deathly afraid of talking in class, then office hours will prove invaluable to you. Here's what I suggest: While you are reading for class, write down or type out questions as they arise. Have one Word document available for taking notes and have another Word document available for writing down questions. When writing down your questions, list the page number that prompted your question. During class, you can use a similar technique; as class goes on, write out a list of questions that arise during class and then, at the end of class, email your professor the list of questions that you noted during class and request a time to meet with him or her. Also, sit in the first row if you are easily distracted by your peers. If you know that you will be distracted by seeing other students online shopping or playing games, then sit in the first row. You will not have anyone in front of you but the professor, and you will not see your classmates' reactions to your questions (not that their reactions should matter).

1. Office Hours

The importance of office hours cannot be overstated. Why? Because your law school exams are not just about the law, but the law according to your specific professor. To that end, if you like using outside materials and supplements, or have a tutor who didn't take a particular course with your professor, you should verify the accuracy of the information you receive from those sources with your professor. The professor is the ultimate authority—and don't you forget it. You are writing your exam for your professor because, after all, the purpose of law school exams is to show the professor that you understand the material as presented. Knowing the law and being able to apply the law are two different things. However, the former without the latter will not assist you in acing law school.

When you visit your professor's office, come prepared. Office hour visits are immensely more productive if you send the professor questions in advance. When doing your reading for class, questions may arise. In my experience, the more detailed the question, the better. You may not even know what questions to ask. I understand. First, make sure you have done the reading. If you have at least done the reading you can ask an intelligible question. Page numbers help you to ask questions when you don't quite know what to ask. For instance, maybe you don't understand "the rule against perpetuities" but don't want to (as you shouldn't) just waltz into your professor's office and say:"I don't understand the rule against perpetuities." Instead, you should say, "Professor, I was reading [insert case name] and didn't understand the court's language contained on pages [insert page numbers]. How does the rule against perpetuities work in this context?"

Sometimes the professor will respond to your questions in writing. This is gold because now you have, in writing, how the professor would explain a particular legal concept. This is likely how you should respond to questions on exams. Write like the professor for the professor.

Now, this is very important. It may be hard for you to evaluate whether or not you are understanding the material. I recall speaking with a student that told me he understood everything the professor said in class, which was why he never visited office hours. That student received less than a 2.5 GPA during his first semester. You are not tested on whether you understand the material in some abstract way. You will be tested on whether you can apply the rules that you have learned in class on a law school examination. Thus, you need to take practice examinations early and often to ensure that you not only understand the rules at play, but can apply them. There is no reason not to go and speak with your professor.

C. Practice Examinations

In order to be really prepared for the exam on game day (game day being test day), you need to practice taking exams. Don't just take practice exams, take them under timed conditions. That way, when you take the actual exam, you will be ready to crush it. When should you start taking practice exams? As early as possible. Personally, I took them two weeks into the semester. By that time, you probably have covered some subtopics for each class. For example, in your contracts course, you will likely cover the elements to an enforceable contract: offer, acceptance, consideration, and certainty. After you cover the concept of making a legally cognizable offer, take practice tests on that topic. Review your notes for an hour or so, and then take several practice exams under timed conditions. That way, you are starting to cement the material and learning what you don't know. The concept of an offer may seem extremely easy to you, but the practice examinations on that topic, which can be found in supplements such as Examples and Explanations, will show you the various ways that your professor can test on the subject. You will also begin to master issue spotting because you will begin to see which facts trigger questions on which subtopics.

After takinga practice test, it is important to compareyour answer to the model answer. If I was confused by an answer provided in a particular supplement, I would take that supplement to my professor and we would discuss my practice answer. I took timed exams with my study partner, who is still my friend to this day. She and I would take the exams under timed conditions and then grade each other's practice exams. This not only kept us accountable, but it allowed us to see how we each approached the questions differently and to discuss the outcome. Before exam day, it is vital that you are clear on what you don't know. The only way to truly discover your learning deficits is by engaging with the material.

Your professor may provide practice exams and/or have supplements that he recommends you purchase. But before purchasing supplements, go to your school's library and see whether it has supplements available for rent. Your library is also a great place to check and see whether your professor has old exams on file that you can use to study. If such exams are available, compile those and save them. Because your professor's past exams are the best indicator of what his or her actual exams will be like, I suggest doing those closest to the exam. If your professor does not have past exams on file, there may be other professors who teach the same subject who have exams on file. Before using exams from other professors, however, ask your professor whether his or her exam is similar to the professor's exam that you found on file. The professor may tell you that the format is different, but the content is helpful. Any advice you get will help. Another thing you can do is ask your professor whether he has sample questions that you can use to practice a particular subject. Don't be shy about asking these questions. You are essentially paying over $100,000 for your legal education, and the professor is there to assist you in learning the law. If it helps, know that I asked all of these questions and more while in school.

If the professor is unresponsive or unhelpful, never fear—supplements to the rescue! There are several supplements that you can use to get sample questions for most first-year and some upper-level courses. For example, if you have a multiple-choice exam, which is rare, the *Glannon Guide* provides solid sample questions.[13] If your exam is written, which is most likely, then I recommend using the *Examples & Explanations* series. Feel free to use a variety of supplements to cre-

---

13 *See* Appendix A for more information on some of my favorite law school supplements and even some information on free supplements!

ate practice exams. I frequently did this to create an exam around the same length as my actual test. For instance, for an exam with fifty multiple choice questions and three long essay exams, I would copy fifty questions from the *Glannon Guide* and seven questions from the *E&E* to create a three-hour exam. Then I would try to complete all of the questions in half the time provided on my actual exam. This helped improve the speed at which I completed exams and ensured that on game day I had enough time to check and proofread my answers. You'd be surprised how many incomplete sentences are left on the pages of an exam because of the compressed time, nerves, and sheer speed of thought. Many professors will not lower your grade for a few grammatical errors here and there, but you want to be sure that the professor can understand your exam and will be able to follow your train of thought. After all, depending on your law school, you may be graded on a curve, which means if there are two exams that both spot the issues, but one is well-written and thus more persuasive, you can probably guess who is going home with the A.

D. Spotting the Issues

The beauty of taking many practice exams is that you get good at issue spotting, which is crucial to your law school success. You can't answer a question if you don't know that it's being asked. Law school exams are unique because you may get a page of facts with a single question at the end, such as "Is there a contract?" You will then be expected to spot and address five to six different issues in answering that single question. For instance, from that one question, you may have six issues such as (1) whether there was an offer, (2) whether the offer was terminated, (3) whether the offer was accepted, (4) whether the statute of frauds prevents the contract, (5) whether there was consideration, and (6) whether the contract's terms were sufficiently definite. Taking practice exams and spotting issues will help you identify the important facts, which are tied to the issues. You should do so many practice exams that when you see a particular fact pattern, you automatically begin to think, "Aha! The professor is testing the statute of frauds." That comes with practice—and often lots of it.

There are people out there who can read the material, digest it, never take a practice test, and then ace the exam. That wasn't me, and likely this book isn't for that person. This book is for people who need to put in the work to get results and who don't mind doing just that—putting in the work. For me, law school was not my backup plan; it was the only plan. I needed to succeed. Failing was not an option, so I did what it took. If you are willing to do what it takes, there is no reason that you cannot succeed in law school.

E. Learn the Law: *The Importance of Rote Memorization*

Rote memorization is a must in law school. Even if your professor's exams are open book, you absolutely must know the law—cold. You also need to understand the law. Understanding the law makes it easier to memorize. So how do you memorize the law? It depends. I liked using a combination of a few different methods.

1. Flashcards

The main way that I memorized the law was through the use of flashcards. You can either use commercial flashcards or make your own flashcards. I used commercial flashcards, but also made my own.

a. *Creating Your Own Flashcards*

Making your own flashcards helps you memorize the rules of law because it takes a significant amount of time to handwrite hundreds of rules of law. This process alone will help you cement the rules to memory. Additionally, unlike commercial flashcards, the flashcards that you create will include rules that were discussed in class by your professor. Those rules should be drafted and memorized using the language your professor used. I had one professor who used PowerPoint presentations during class. This professor posted her slides online for us to use while studying. This was great because I was then able to make flashcards based on my professor's recitation of the law. I recommend making your own flashcards because then you can customize your flashcards to your professor. Remember, there's contracts, and then there's contracts as taught, understood, and tested by your professor. To ace your exam, you want to memorize the law as tested by your professor.

Moreover, when you make your own flashcards you can create some that list key cases you should know. This is particularly important for classes such as constitutional law. I missed an entire page on my constitutional law exam (please flip through every page of the exam before starting the exam), but I still received an A– in the class because I cited cases in my answer. This is not necessary, but if you start studying early and have a good grasp of the black-letter law (i.e., the basic rules of law for a particular subject), then I suggest you begin memorizing case names, key facts, and rules of law. Why? Because this will allow you to persuasively draft an essay response. When writing a motion for an actual court case, citations are everything. If you craft an essay response that correctly states the law and demonstrates a similar fact pattern to a case discussed in class, it will only strengthen your exam answer. Again, this is to ensure you excel to the highest level. Thus, making your own flashcards is extremely useful for both learning the law as recited by your professor and learning about key cases and holdings that were discussed in class.

If you are going to make flashcards, use them. You should have a set of flashcards with you on the train, in the car, wherever you may have an idle five or 10 minutes so that you are using your time wisely. Do not think that the process of making flashcards alone will prepare you for exam day. Making flashcards takes a lot of time. I think it's helpful to make five to ten flashcards, then spend five to ten minutes going through those cards before moving on to the next set. Why? If you are simply writing down the law without actively engaging with the material, you may end up wasting time. Every action, even creating your study materials, presents an opportunity for you to engage with the material.

You have to make sure you are actually retaining the information that you are studying. If, while creating flashcard after flashcard, you find yourself drifting off to sleep or robotically writing out flashcards without thinking about what you are writing, stop, and start studying a different way. For instance, maybe you need to write out 10 flashcards and then do a hypothetical, using one of the many law school supplements recommended in Appendix A. You do yourself a disservice by studying for ten hours when you may be the type of person that can only retain information and actively engage for four hours. You must know your limits and listen to your body. There will be many "C" students who spend the night in the law library. It's not about the quantity of time you spend studying, but about the quality of your study time.

b. Commercial Flashcards

I recommend using commercial flashcards in combination with the flashcards that you create yourself. There is no shortcut to the top and creating your own may be the best way for you to retain the material. There were concepts on exams that I am convinced were not fully explained in class. However, commercial flashcards do a great job presenting *all* the information needed to understand a subject. The downside is that sometimes you don't cover all of that information in class. Basically, commercial flashcards may contain *more* law than you need to know for an exam, and your time is limited. To save time, consider reviewing the index included within a pack of commercial flashcards, compare that index to your course syllabus, and only study the topics listed on your syllabus. Better yet, ask your professor whether a particular topic covered by the commercial flashcards (but not on your syllabus) will appear on the exam. There's no shame in asking. Also, you should know that your professor may not cover everything on the exam in class, which is why it is imperative that you read everything assigned by your professor. You have to study smart, and wasting time learning everything about contracts when your test covers only 25 percent of the topic does not make sense. Commercial flashcards also help you to check whether you fully understand a topic. Some commercial flashcards, in addition to displaying the law, contain practice questions, which will test your knowledge of the black-letter law. As previously stated, do not memorize the law without knowing how to apply it. Knowing how to apply the law in combination with knowing the rules will help you succeed on exam day. Learn how to apply the law, and then memorize it. Flashcards can help with the memorization, but practice tests will help with the application.

c.   Writing the Law

Another way to memorize the law is to write it—over and over and over again. This was helpful to me when memorizing the law, especially when I wasn't at home or near a library. You can do this anywhere; if you're in the car for thirty minutes to an hour, just take a sheet of paper and write a rule of law over and over until it is cemented in your mind. You don't need many materials to do this. You just need something to write on and something to write with. This is a simple task, and an effective one.

d.   Listening to the Law

Some bar prep companies provide study materials to first-year (1L) law students. Those study aids sometimes come with online access to lectures on many 1L course subjects, such as contracts, constitutional law, civil procedure, torts, ethics, evidence and property. If you commute to school, or even walk to school, these lectures are a great way to study on the go. I would frequently listen to these lectures while on the way to class. It helped me begin memorizing and retaining the law. Also, different lecturers explained the material differently. If you didn't understand the statute of frauds from your professor, you may understand it better from another lecturer. The more exposure you have to the law, the easier it becomes to grasp and apply legal concepts. You should always seek opportunities to study. I don't suggest studying 24/7, but rather use moments that would have otherwise been wasted to study.

F. Study Groups: It Depends—Who Do You Trust?

I don't recommend study groups for everyone, but they can be helpful. One question you should ask yourself before joining a study group is "Have I ever successfully participated in a study group before?" This question is important because if you have, then it may work for you, but if you haven't, then you may not learn best in group settings. I preferred having a study partner as opposed to a study group, and we would really push each other. That's the other thing: Your study group or study partner should have the same academic goals as you—to get A's. A person studying to get all A's undoubtedly studies differently (harder) than a person just trying to pass. Attitude is contagious and determines a lot. If you decide to study in a group, it must be a group of people all seeking to get A's and excel in the course, and ideally a group of people who want everyone in the group to excel as well. I can honestly say that my study partner and I both had similar goals: to transfer to a top law school, get all A's and obtain positions in BigLaw.[14] This helped us push each other.

Now, when selecting your study group, you want to think about whether you trust everyone in the group. You don't need to trust them with your life—this isn't *Survivor*—but you do want to trust them enough to be vulnerable in front of them. You have to get rid of your ego a bit to excel in law school. I became very comfortable saying "I don't know" in law school. For the group to work, you must be able to tell one another when help is needed, because ideally your group will become your support system.What you don't know, someone else may be able to teach you, and vice versa. Additionally, you must be able to trust that your group members won't make you feel inferior for lacking knowledge on a particular topic. You need a group that will lift you up, not tear you down. Your group should also be willing to share resources, study aids, and notes. The goal has to be that everyone in the group does well. I found my study partner because we were both sitting in the first row of class and we both asked questions during class. From there, I asked her if she wanted

---

14 As a reminder, "BigLaw" is just a colloquial nickname for the largest law firms in the nation. Most of these firms pay the "market" starting salary to new associate attorneys, which, when I started was $160,000. That starting salary has since increased. Not too shabby – right?

to study together and she agreed. The rest is history. Our first semester, we received very similar grades and became great friends. We are still close to this day.

Study groups often fail due to disorganization and too much socializing. The most effective groups have a blueprint for what the group plans to study. That strategy should be discussed prior to meeting. When I wasn't studying one-on-one with my study partner, I would study with a small group of three classmates that I trusted. Before meeting with my study group, I or another study group member would email out the plan for our study session. Normally, the person that organizes the study group sends out the plan and takes ownership of organizing the group session —at least for the first session. The study plan would usually include which topics we planned to cover and for how long. If, for example, we planned to study constitutional law, the group leader would inform the group prior to meeting that everyone should review the constitutional requirements for standing before the study session so that during the session we can test one another on standing. For our sessions, everyone in the study group would be required to bring two to five essay hypotheticals to the study session and during the session we would take timed practice essay exams, switch papers, and review each other's work and ask one another questions. Do you now see why you need to trust your study group? Study groups are ineffective when you don't trust (or like) one another. Would you want to admit that you have no clue what is going on in class to someone you didn't trust? Would you be comfortable with that person reviewing your work? Probably not. Choose your study group wisely and don't feel overly committed to the group. If you try a study group early on in the semester and it does not work for you, feel free to leave the group and study on your own or try studying with a partner versus a group.

Another note: Because my study partner and I wanted to make sure we were on the same page, there were times when questions would arise during our study sessions and we would write them down and, you guessed it, take them to our professor (we were in the same classes). This was helpful because, as you can imagine, law students can have strong personalities, and you don't want to spend 50 percent of your study time debating whether you or your study partner has the right interpretation of a particular statute. Just ask your professor. Overall, you should trust your gut when it comes to who you should study with and try to find someone that you (1) like, (2) work well with, and (3) know works hard. Who knows, you may even make a lifelong friend.

"Those at the top of the mountain didn't fall there."
—*Marcus Washling*

CHAPTER VI.

IT WILL TAKE MORE THAN GOOD GRADES

During your first year of law school, your primary responsibility will be to get good grades. However, there are some other things that you can do (besides studying) to position yourself for a successful legal career.

A. Character and Fitness

Prior to law school, I knew that to become a lawyer I had to take the bar examination, but I had no idea that I would also be required to take a character and fitness test before being admitted to the state bar. To become an attorney, you will need to demonstrate that you have good moral character and are fit to practice law. You demonstrate such strong character by passing a character and fitness test. The character and fitness test is a long background check to make sure that you have acted somewhat ethically throughout your life—and by "life," I mean your entire life. As with everything else in law school, you must pay to complete this process. Some jurisdictions offer a discount for starting your character and fitness application during your first year of law school. The character and fitness test is extensive. You are required to submit all of your prior addresses and a complete list of every job you have ever held in your life. You need to provide a copy of your driving record, criminal record, and school disciplinary history (if applicable). Some of this information you will have readily available, but it is more likely that you will need to gather documents to complete this process. Be extremely forthcoming with the character and fitness committee and get your affairs in order. Also, if you have a criminal record (misdemeanor or felony), you want to know as early as possible if your background will prohibit you from taking the bar exam, and the earlier you communicate with your counselor—the person assigned to review your character and fitness file—and get them what they need, the better.[15] If you have delinquencies on

---

15 If you have a criminal record, do not freak out. Studies show that one in three Americans has at least some criminal record, so you are not alone. The key to passing the character and fitness examination with a criminal record is being 100% honest on the application and having all of your documentation. Even if your record is sealed or expunged, you have to report it to the Character and Fitness examiners. Also, make sure that you are honest about your record on your law school application; I have heard horror stories of law school graduates being unable to practice because they lied on their law school application and subsequently the Character and Fitness examiners found out. Honesty is key and 100% candor is required. I know plenty of people with criminal records that have passed the character and fitness portion of the exam.

your credit report or unpaid parking tickets, you will want to pay all of that prior to applying or be able to prove that you are on a payment plan, in good standing. Now do you see why handling this early makes sense? I have heard horror stories of law school graduates having their swearing in ceremony delayed because they waited until the last minute to complete the character and fitness application.

B. Networking

In addition to completing some of the administrative paperwork necessary to practice law, you should begin developing relationships with practitioners. That's right, you should start networking early— before you need anything. People who say they hate networking are more than likely saying that they hate going to crowded events and trying to get the cards of the power players in the room, but that is not networking; that's collecting business cards. Networking consists of building relationships with people—real relationships, which means that it takes time and will not happen during one event. The best networking advice that I can give you is to network before you need it. Most lawyers would be happy to speak with a budding attorney about their careers and how they navigated the legal profession. You may think it's odd to cold-call someone in hopes of receiving career advice, but it's not as uncommon as you think. This is a profession—a community of professionals who mostly want to see incoming attorneys do well. I get calls and emails from law students I have never met, and I don't have a problem speaking with them. When I was a student, lawyers took time out of their busy days to speak with me—and now I get to return the favor.

As a law student, your primary focus is on succeeding in law school, but your ultimate goal in going to law school is not just to graduate but to have a successful career, legal or otherwise. Unfortunately, in many instances law school does not teach you how to practice. Some of your law professors might have never practiced law. Therefore, it is important that you speak with as many practitioners as possible during law school to learn about the practice of law. You will benefit from learning all you can about the different types of legal practices out there. After all, during law school you are likely still learning what type of law you will find interesting. Are you interested in working in the private or public sector? Do you know the difference? Are you interested in focusing on a particular area of the law? To answer these questions, it is helpful to speak with practicing attorneys.

1. Bar Associations

Bar association meetings are a great place to meet lawyers. Bar associations are professional associations—clubs—for lawyers and those within the legal profession. Some of you may be the first in your family to attend law school. Joining a bar association would allow you the opportunity to develop relationships with lawyers. Lawyers (and law students) often join bar associations to network and learn from lawyers with similar interests. Bar associations can be likened to student groups. In college, there was a student group for almost everyone. Likewise, there is a bar association for almost everyone. Some bar associations focus on certain areas of the law and others provide spaces for different minority groups. For example, many cities and states have bar associations specifically for certain racial and ethnic groups. Law students often receive reduced or free membership dues while in law school so you should take full advantage and join bar associations that interest you.

In law school, I knew (or thought I knew) that I wanted to practice employment law, so I attended bar association meetings on various employment law topics. This not only allowed me to meet other employment law attorneys, but it helped me narrow down what specifically interested me in the employment law field. After all, what did I really know about the law on my first day of law school? Looking back, I'd venture to say not much. Furthermore (and this was an unexpected benefit), spending time with practitioners helped me start speaking like a lawyer. It also caused me to see lawyers as regular relatable people. It is so easy, as a law student, to put practitioners on an unreasonably high pedestal, but attending bar association meetings, where I was often the only student, helped me to see lawyers as "normal" and kind people. Many of the volunteer bar associations will have both professional meetings, covering new trends in the law, and social events, where you can relax, network, and really start building relationships with the members of the association. Take advantage of both the professional and social settings that bar associations provide.

Maybe you're thinking you don't have time to network because studying will consume all of your time and attention. That may be true for you, and you should do whatever it takes to be successful in your studies—after all, getting good grades is one of your primary goals. If you want to network but you are concerned about time management, try to find a local bar association that hosts meetings near your law school during the lunch hour. Try to attend at least one of those meetings every month. You would likely have to eat lunch anyway; now, your lunch break can be even more productive. You may even be the only law student there, which will undoubtedly impress those in attendance. You will be showing initiative and showing that you don't mind going above and beyond. Who knows, you may even meet your future employer by attending a bar association meeting. In addition to simply attending meetings, you can always volunteer to work an event or two. The key to joining the association is not just to attend, but for you to start developing relationships, as well as your personal brand.

2. Alumni

Another great way to begin networking is to reach out to alumni of your law school. Ask to be placed on the alumni listserv or talk to your alumni office about volunteering at an alumni event. Alumni are always great to connect with because there is an instant commonality between you and them. Additionally, many large national law firms' websites have a search function that permits you to filter by their attorneys' law schools and undergraduate institutions. Search by both to find alumni of your law school and potentially your undergraduate institution. Go to the website of a firm that you are interested in, search for alumni of your current law school and/or undergraduate institution, and then send an email asking for a brief call or coffee to learn about his or her career trajectory. Below is a sample email that I've previously used:

Ms. _____:

I noticed that you graduated from Northwestern University Pritzker School of Law. I am currently a student at Northwestern. Do you have time to meet for a 30-minute coffee or would you be able to have a 15-minute phone call regarding your career trajectory? In the event that you are willing to speak with me, I am available on the below dates and times:

- Tuesday, March 15th at 3:30 pm
- Friday, March 10th at 10:00 am
- Monday, March 8th at 4:00 pm

I am happy to schedule our meeting directly with your assistant. Please let me know what works best for you. Thank you for your time.

Best regards,

Ashley

You can edit the above sample as you see fit, but here are some things to keep in mind: (1) ensure the first line includes the common link between you and the person you are emailing, (2) include dates and times that you are available, and (3) keep it short.

Ensure the first line illustrates the commonality between you and the lawyer. If you are emailing an alumnus of your school, be sure to note that you attend and/or graduated from the same school as the person you are emailing. Likewise, if the commonality is that you and the attorney are from the same hometown, note that. Bottom line, be sure to build commonality within the first line of the email. What if you don't have anything in common with the lawyer? In that case, be sure to state why you are emailing: "I noticed that you practice employment law. I am interested in the employment law field. Do you have fifteen minutes to speak with me about your career trajectory?"

Include dates and times that you are available for a meeting. Either within your first email or after the attorney responds, include three dates and times that you are available and offer to coordinate schedules with the attorney's assistant. When coming up with a location, offer to meet either at their office or at a coffee shop near their office. Look up available locations near their office. Bottom line, make it very easy for the attorney to meet with you. Then, once a date is confirmed, send a calendar invitation.

Keep it short. Your initial email to an attorney you don't know is not the proper forum to tell your life story. Your goal in sending this email is narrow: you want to schedule a time to speak with the attorney either in-person or over the phone. I am of the mind that it is easier to connect in-person versus over the phone or via email, but lawyers have limited time and you want to be respectful of their time, which is why your email should always be concise and have a specific request. What do you want the lawyer to do after reading your email? Well, you want them to agree to meet with you. Include a call to action in your email. For the first meeting, I always suggest requesting either coffee or a 15-minute phone conversation. Why fifteen minutes? Because it's short—and honestly, who doesn't have fifteen minutes? I mean, seriously, that's not a huge ask. Time for lawyers is often precious because in many instances lawyers are billing for every minute of their time. When a lawyer has to bill, that means they must account for every minute of their day on a time sheet—it is as bad as it sounds. Therefore, it is a good practice for you to preemptively show that you value the attorney's time by giving them the option of either a short coffee or a call. Again, the goal here is to set the meeting. Get it on the books so you can make the initial connection and start to build a professional relationship.

Once your initial meeting is scheduled, research the person with whom you are scheduled to meet. There are three key ways to research attorneys: (1) Google; (2) LinkedIn; and (3) their firm's website. Verify, however, that the information you find (particularly via Google) is directly applicable to the attorney you are meeting with – if you are unsure, disregard the information found. There are a lot of lawyers in the world, and some of them have the same name, so be careful. When searching Google, you are essentially looking to see whether the attorney has won any awards, won a big case, etc. You are not looking for invasive personal information about the attorney— professional information only. When searching an attorney on LinkedIn, you are looking to see their employment history and any volunteer causes with which they are publicly affiliated. Many attorneys have worked for more than one firm. When you meet with them you can ask what prompted them to leave one firm and go to another so that you can begin to develop your opinion about different firms. When searching an attorney on their firm's website, you are looking to understand what type of law they practice so that you are asking appropriate questions during your meeting. And, regardless of whether you are searching LinkedIn, Google, or their firm's website, always keep an eye out for commonalities between you and the attorney.

In preparation for your meeting, write down your questions in advance. This is, after all, your meeting. Some basic questions to help you get started are below:

- Why did you decide to go to law school?
- What led you to practice **[insert type of law here]**?
- How did you decide between transactional law and litigation?
- Is there something you wish you had done in law school that you did not do for one reason or another?
- What advice would you give your younger, law school, self?
- I am interested in **[insert type of law here]**. How do you suggest I approach a career in that field?
- Is there anyone else that you recommend I speak with about **[insert type of law here]**?
- If I have other questions in the future, is it okay if I reach out to you again?

Remember, people want to help people they like. Show your personality! Be gracious and don't argue with the advice given. If you ask for advice and the attorney gives you advice, be grateful. After all, you asked for their opinion.

Hopefully the above strategies have shown you that everyone in law school can develop a network of lawyers. And even if you don't have any lawyers in your family, consider asking your family members if they work with or know any lawyers that might not mind speaking with you.

Develop your networking plan and stick with it. Set goals. Try to meet one new attorney per month, whether that be an alumnus of your law school or an attorney you meet via a bar association meeting. This is your career and you have to take ownership over it. The grades are important, but building relationships is also extremely important.

The strategies above will help you to set initial meetings with attorneys, but developing professional relationships requires you to followup. After you have made a connection, it is important that you set reminders to followup every three months or whenever you have something to update them on. When I received my grades, I would let my mentors know how I performed during the semester and we would often discuss my goals for summer employment. If you are uncomfortable sharing your grades with your mentors, you can set Google alerts for companies or topics that may interest your contacts.If their firm is in the news for moving to a new office space, you can send them the article with a note that says, "Congrats on the move!" It takes time to build relationships so don't rush it, but be consistent and try to network with people that you genuinely like. There's nothing more frustrating than pulling teeth during a conversation. I do not suggest trying desperately to build a relationship with an attorney that is clearly not interested in mentoring you. There's a reason that you have the friends that you have now. You all likely connect and make each other's lives better. The same should be true of your professional network. Also, you should always look for ways to help those in your network. Learn whether your mentors are seeking to adjunct at a law school or whether they are seeking a law student to help them with an article they want to publish. Maybe you can't volunteer, but you can send an email out to your classmates to see if anyone is interested. Many people network to get something out of the relationship, but before you look for what you can get, you should try to add to the relationship. Trust me; even as a law student, there are ways you can contribute to your network.

"Things may come to those who wait, but only the things left by those who hustle."
—*Unknown*

CHAPTER VII.

LAND THE JOB YOU WANT

Getting good grades and developing a strong network can help you to land full-time post-graduate employment, but you also need a good understanding of the legal market. Before we jump headfirst into how to land a job, there are some key terms you should add to your vocabulary as it relates to law school employment. There are various types of jobs you can obtain in law school, each of which comes with its own set of rules and hiring processes.

A. Summer Associate Positions

Summer associate positions are typically high-paying summer internships at large law firms that can offer the possibility, at the end of the summer, of a full-time offer to join the firm after graduation. Large firms do the majority of their hiring from their summer classes. I worked as a summer associate twice at two different firms, and both firms made full-time offers to all of the 2L summer associates. As a 1L summer associate I was offered the opportunity to return as a 2L summer associate and potentially receive a full-time job offer. This is typical, as most 1L summer associates do not received full-time job offers without spending at least some time at the firm for a second summer.

It is important to note that working as a summer associate is one of the most lucrative jobs you can have while in law school. As a 1L summer associate, I made a little more than $2,000 a week. As a 2L summer associate, I fared even better, coming in at around $3,000 a week. Many large firms pay their summer associates the same weekly salary as their first-year associates. If the market rate is $190,000 year, summer associates receive the weekly prorated equivalent of that annual salary. Not too shabby. For me, since admittedly I hadn't been bringing in the big bucks pre–law school, I replaced close to 80 percent of the full-time salary I earned in a year before law school in only ten weeks as a summer associate. Not bad.

Summer associates' activities will vary greatly based on the size, practice area, and location of the firm, but in general they work with partners and associates on discrete projects. At the end of the summer, they are evaluated on their performance on those projects and often receive reviews from the partners and associates with whom they work. The projects will vary greatly and may include researching legal issues, drafting small sections of motions, summarizing deposition transcripts, or helping out with pro bono cases. Many summer associates also have an opportunity to shadow attorneys in court.In addition to working, summer associates often attend weekly lunches, breakfasts, and other fun summer events. I recall attending a different lunch or event every other day during my summer associate experiences.

If, after law school, you plan to work at a large law firm, then your goal should be to obtain a summer associate position as early as possible. Large firms complete the vast majority of their entry-level hiring from their summer associate classes. Sure, you may be able to move laterally into a large firm from some other job later in your career, but why take the risk when you don't have to do so? The best way to ensure you are walking across that graduation stage with a job at a large firm is to obtain a summer associate position after either your 1L or 2L year.

Because of the pay, perks, and high probability of obtaining an offer of full-time employment, summer associate positions are unsurprisingly hard to obtain. Large firms are seeking candidates with outstanding grades from the nation's top law schools. Still, exceptions always exist, and if you don't fall into a firm's traditional recruiting category (great grades from a top school), don't give up! Network and apply!

To find out which firms traditionally hire for those exclusive 1L summer associate positions, work with your career services department. Furthermore, if you are a minority law student, several firms offer 1L diversity scholarships that include not only a scholarship but also a 1L summer associate position! Use Google to discover which firms in your area offer 1L summer associate positions. A simple Google search for "1L summer associate positions Chicago" may lead you to a list of summer associate positions available in Illinois. If you are open to relocating, search for positions not only in your area but also within the surrounding cities where you are willing to work. Some firms offer 1L summer positions in some offices and not others. Also, remember that this can change from yeartoyear, meaning that firms that offered 1L positions when I was in law school very well may not offer 1L summer associate positions currently. Do your research.

One consideration to note about 1L summer associate positions is that unlike 2L summer associate positions, 1L positions traditionally do not conclude with you receiving an offer of full-time employment, but rather an offer to work as a 2L summer associate the following summer. The benefit of this arrangement might not, at first, be apparent, but firms (and companies too) like hiring sought-after candidates. Therefore, starting your 2L summer job search already having an offer to join a reputable firm can help you to obtain additional offers for your 2L summer. Why would you interview at additional firms if you already have an offer to go back to your 1L firm? Well, law firms, like law schools, are ranked against each other. Some would argue that working at the highest-ranked firm you can right out of law school can only help to propel your career in the future. The truth is, unlike what you may hear on-campus, all law firms are not created equal. Law firms are very different in terms of the resources offered, the bonuses paid, the experiences that associates receive and the overall culture. You should research law firms just like you researched law schools. For firm research, there are various online resources available such as Above the Law, The American Lawyer, Vault, and Chambers Associate, just to name a few. Each year, The American Lawyer comes out with a list of the top 200 law firms in the nation. This list is commonly referred to as the AmLaw200 and ranks firms using various criteria. Feel free to look at this list and get a sense of how many of the firms on this list are in your city. This will help you to learn about some of the most profitable law firms in your city. Again, this is your career. The more information you have about the market and the players, the better.

B. Internships

Legal internships can take many forms. These are summer positions at either a firm or a company where you work for the summer. But similar to summer associates, legal interns may spend a great deal of time conducting legal research, drafting motions for court, interacting with clients, shadowing lawyers, and working on pro bono activities. Most internships do not come with the expectation of full-time employment at the end of the summer, and the organization of an internship will vary greatly from company to company. Furthermore, there is no standard pay for legal interns. Legal interns are typically paid an hourly rate that can vary greatly based on the company.

C. Externships

Externships are unpaid legal internships in the public sector where a student receives course credit for the work performed. Externs work either full or part-time during the school year or over the summer. One very common externship is a judicial externship, where law students can work for federal or state court judges researching and writing drafts of judicial opinions. Judicial externships are fantastic opportunities to learn more about the judicial system, build relationships with judges, and learn whether you have an interest in serving as a judicial law clerk after law school. As a judicial extern, you get only a small taste of life as a judicial law clerk, but it is a great experience nonetheless. Externships are great to complete during the school year so you can spend your summer working for a firm or agency that may give you an offer of full-time employment.Judicial law clerks are full-time permanent or temporary employees of federal or state courts. Law clerks help judges manage their caseloads by writing opinions and organizing the judges' dockets. Federal clerkships are very selective and difficult to obtain. Many firms pay federal law clerks special bonuses for completing clerkships before joining the firm full-time.

D. Law Clerks

Working at a firm as a law clerk typically means that you do what the firm needs you to do on an hourly basis. Law firms of all sizes employ law clerks both during the school year and over the summer. Law clerk positions are essentially part-time jobs at law firms. These positions can lead to full-time employment but traditionally do not carry the expectation of such an offer. When I worked as a law clerk, it was simply to get my foot in the door at a law firm. I worked at a small employment law firm during my first year of law school for about $10 an hour. My job was essentially to complete intake interviews. I answered the phone when potential clients called and asked them a series of questions that helped the attorneys determine whether the firm should pursue a particular case. It was simple, but I learned a lot and had something to discuss in my 1L summer associate interviews. Otherwise, my pre–law school work (i.e. my full-time employment before law school) was not directly relevant to the legal field. Having some legal work experience, even if it wasn't very substantive, helped during the on-campus interviewing process.

E. Fellowships

Fellowships are positions at either public agencies or law firms. Law firm fellowships do not carry the expectation of an offer of full-time employment at the end of the summer. Other than that, however, a law firm fellowship may be similar to a summer associate position. Some government fellowships are paid. Some fellows receive small stipends for completing a summer's worth of legal work for a particular government agency. Also, government fellows who have their 711 may be able to handle actual cases. A 711 law license is a valuable way for law students to gain in-court experience. To receive a 711 license, most jurisdictions require a law student to have completed one-half of the total credits needed to graduate and be in good academic standing. A 711 can only be used to work for a qualified legal aid bureau, government agency, or legal clinic. Furthermore, there are post-graduation full-time fellowships available that are typically for a period of one, two, or five years. Fellowships are a great way to get experience, and there are a wide variety of fellowships available.

F. Develop a Career Action Plan

Develop a career action plan and note the key application deadlines in your calendar. You want to be sure you do not lose an opportunity because you missed the deadline. Speak to your career counselor as soon as possible to get feedback on your career goals and plans. Full disclosure: Career counselors get a bad rap in some law schools. Their job is not to find you a job; it's to help you through the job search process. With that in mind, seek their feedback on your résumé. Ask them if they know any students who work at the firm at which you are interviewing. Have specific tasks that they can help you with and ask them detailed questions, but remember that it is up to you to find your job. Furthermore, speak with your mentors and other legal professionals in the field about your job search and your career plan.

A career calendar is an action plan that lists tasks you need to complete before applying to legal jobs and also includes deadlines for legal internships, fellowships, and summer associate positions for which you seek to apply. A sample 1L career action plan is included below:

DATE	TASK	STATUS
October 15	Complete résumé	*In progress*
October 30	Have résumé reviewed by career counselor, legal mentor, and colleague	*Not started*
December 1	Apply to 1L summer associate positions	*Not started*

DATE	TASK	STATUS
December 15	Complete character and fitness bar application	*In progress*
April 15	Register for regional and local career fairs	*Not started*
July 30/ongoing	Apply to full-time federal and/or judicial clerkships	*Not started*

Your action plan can also include key school-related test and study dates, but I definitely recommend at a minimum having a career action plan. Feel free to update your action plan with deadlines for specific firm jobs/internships. The above is simply a general example to help you get started. Also, to put yourself in the best position possible, apply early. You may want to note in your career action plan the date that the application opens, in addition to the deadline to apply. I have heard horror stories of firms passing on a candidate because he or she waited to apply until the last day that the application was due. You want to appear eager and ready to work. Think of the job hunt like dating: No one wants someone nobody else wants, and no one wants to be another person's sloppy seconds. Even if a firm is not your first choice, treat all firms as though they are your top pick! After you receive all of your offers, that's the time to be selective, but before that, give each firm the impression that you would work there for the long haul.

G. Getting Interviews

You want to interview at several places, which means you must apply to several different places. First, develop a list of internships, fellowships, and summer associate positions for which you plan to apply. Then, start using LinkedIn or the organization's website to identify current employees you can speak with about the organization, its summer program, and how best to obtain an interview. Because you will likely start applying in December of your first year of law school, develop this list early and start meeting people right away. There is nothing stopping you from developing a list of employers before you even start law school. Next, you will need to start preparing your application materials—this may include a writing sample, cover letter, résumé, and transcript. In developing your list of potential summer jobs, be sure to list the application requirements in an Excel spreadsheet so that you can easily reference it in the future and ensure that you have everything you need to apply. Find out whether the employer will need an official or unofficial transcript. If they need an official transcript, find out whether you can submit all other materials in advance of your transcript and preorder your transcript to be sent to the organization immediately once it's available. If you plan ahead, you shouldn't have a problem completing all of your applications in a timely fashion, but if you don't plan, it is easy to become overwhelmed and miss out on opportunities.

H. Interviewing

Please complete practice interviews before actually interviewing. Practice makes perfect, and trust me, it will never hurt to over-prepare. During my years as a career counselor, I discovered that a lot of people believe they are great interviewees when in fact they are not. Legal interviews can take many forms, so there is really no such thing as a traditional legal interview. Some interviewers simply look at your résumé and ask you questions about your résumé from top to bottom.Other interviewerswill ask you a variety of questions based on hypotheticals to determine how you respond in certain situations.Some legal interviews will consist of behavioral questions, which start with "Tell me about a time when…." Other interviewers may simply ask you whether you have any questions for them at the outset of the interview and expect you to ask questions about the firm for the entire interview. Basically, you will likely encounter a wide variety of interview formats, which makes practice even more important.

Preparation is key. Once you've received an interview, the work does not stop. You should prepare for your interview by first looking up the company and or organization. Does the organization have a LinkedIn or Facebook page? If so, look at those as well. After you have a feel for what the organization does, look up your interviewers. If you don't know who they are, see if you can connect with one of the most junior people at the organization to ask them for their advice before your interview. I would typically send the following short email to junior associates after receiving an interview at his or her firm:

Ms. _____:

I noticed from your firm biography that you recently graduated from Northwestern University Pritzker School of Law. I currently attend Northwestern and recently received an interview with your firm. Would you mind having a 15-minute phone call with me regarding your interview experience? My interview takes place on Friday, July 15th. Any advice you can offer will be greatly appreciated.

Best regards,

Ashley

Most associates I contacted would respond quickly and hop on a phone call, but some did not. Send the email to a few (three or four) different junior associates, you only need one or two to respond.

"When you're winning, keep competing like you're losing."
—*Unknown*

CHAPTER VIII.

2L YEAR FOCUSES ON EMPLOYMENT: STAY HUNGRY

Congrats! You made it to your second year of law school. You're excited, anxious, and more than likely getting ready for on-campus interviewing, better known as OCI. This is an important step in your law school process, particularly if you plan to work at a large law firm after law school. Most large law firms hire the vast majority of new associates through the OCI process. What does that mean to you? That means that you may land your full-time job with only one full year of law school under your belt. Sounds crazy, right? So, how you prepare for OCI matters…A LOT.

A. On-Campus Interviewing (OCI)

Let me reiterate again what you're likely tired of hearing: There is no substitute for having stellar grades. You can interview well, look the part, and sound great, but at the end of the day, grades are king in law school. The first thing you will want to do before deciding where you will apply is look at your grades and speak with your career counselor about which firms you will be competitive for based on your specific profile. This will help you narrow down your list. There are a lot of firms that exist. The goal is not to apply to all of them and see which ones stick. The goal is to apply to firms that want you just as much as you want them—and hopefully those firms will also be great places to work that will treat you with some level of respect. You will also want to present yourself well! During OCI, I completed more than twenty interviews and handed each firm a packet of information containing my résumé, a cover letter, a letter of recommendation, and my transcript. Each sheet of paper was placed in a sheet protector, and the cover page of each packet listed my name and the firm's name. For example, I would place my materials in a booklet like the one pictured below, and the cover page would say, "Ashley's [Insert Firm Name Here] Application Materials."

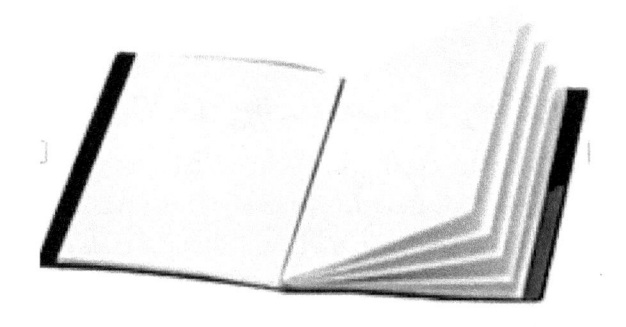

1. But My School Doesn't Have OCI!

Not all schools will have a robust OCI interviewing event. In fact, many law schools (ranked outside of the T-14) do not have hundreds of firms on campus to interview during the OCI period. Given that, it may make sense to make a list of fifty to a hundred firms in which you have interest and mass-mail them your application packet, including your cover letter (tailored to the firm), résumé, transcript, and writing sample. You may be thinking that mass mailing one hundred law firms sounds like a ton of work. Well, you're right, but at least you will know you put forth a concerted effort in your job search. How can you complete that many applications and still study? Consistency. It's not as hard as you think. If you mail your application to ten firms a day for ten days, you can quickly apply to one hundred firms. In short, if your school does not have a robust OCI process, you can still make sure that you are presenting yourself well to a wide variety of firms. But the grind doesn't stop at applying; after all, the goal is to land some interviews.

2. Additional Interviewing Tips

You should do practice interviews—and a lot of them! And by "a lot," I mean that you should do at least five mock interviews before you have your first "real" interview. I promise you it won't take as much time as you think. And I recommend you conduct mock interviews through different means: over Skype, via phone, in person. Why? Because you never know how your initial interview will take place—whether it takes place over the phone, via Skype, or in person, you will be ready!

In addition, below are some tips that you can employ to perform well during your interview:

1. **Know what the firm practices and what it doesn't**. There is nothing more embarrassing than telling your interviewer that you seek to practice entertainment law when the firm for which you are interviewing does not have that practice. Make sure you know, at minimum, what type of law firm you are interviewing with. Is it a full-service firm, a boutique firm, or a specialty firm, where all of the attorneys practice the same thing? You have to know what the firm does and what it is known in the market for doing exceptionally well.

2. **Write down the top three reasons you should be hired and why you are the best fit for the prospective firm**. Interviews can be long—really long—and at times you, as the interviewee, can forget to tell the interviewer *why* they should hire you. Specifically, you want to convey some of your most impressive accomplishments—those that show the interviewer why you are the ideal candidate. I recommend writing down your top three accomplishments and looking at them before your interview so that you do not forget to

talk about them in the interview.

3. **Research your interviewer**. You should know the publicly available information about your interviewer's professional experience—no need to look for their baby pictures or personal information. But look up his or her LinkedIn profile and firm biography. This is helpful for two reasons: (1) you want to know what your interviewer practices so that you can ask specific questions about said practice, and (2) you want to build commonality with your interviewer.

4. **Make the connection**. When researching your interviewer, look for things that you might have in common with him or her. Did you attend the same school, grow up in the same town, or play the same collegiate sport? Be sure to bring up commonalities early (if you can sneak it into the conversation without being creepy). For example, it would be perfectly acceptable to say, "I have been looking forward to meeting you. I saw that you played high school tennis, so did I. Do you still play?" You want the interviewer to have a good experience with you and remember you after a long day of interviewing multiple candidates. When interviewing, I print off the LinkedIn profile and firm biography of my interviewer and highlight all commonalities. For instance, if

we attended the same school—law school, undergraduate institution, or high school—I highlight it and, in the interview, find a (non-creepy) way to bring it up to build commonality.

5. **Tell the interviewer why you want to work for their firm specifically**. When you are asked, "What are you looking for in a firm?", you need to answer with why you are looking to work for the firm for which you are interviewing in detail. One great way to answer this question is to say, "I spoke with Sandy, a second-year associate at your firm. She explained that during the summer, summer associates receivethree firm mentors and conduct a mock trial. I would love to have those experiences during my summer with a firm, which is why your firm is my first choice." You want to show that you have a contact at the firm that has convinced you that working there is the right decision for your career. You want to avoid giving an answer that is too general.

6. **Have a set of questions ready to go**. Don't be the person who has no questions for the interviewer. You want to have some questions ready to go, but make sure that your interviewer can actually answer your questions. Don't just ask questions about a random firm award you read about on the website because, quite frankly, your inter-

viewer may not know about the firm's most recent award. Below are some good questions to ask in a pinch, but the best questions will be those specific to your interviewer.

a. What is one thing that you love about working here and one thing you would change if you could?

b. How is performance measured in the first year of practice? Are there annual reviews or semiannual reviews, etc.?

c. How did you select your practice area?

d. When you think of people that perform best at the firm, what is one characteristic that they all share?

Now, not everyone will interview at a law firm, but similar principles apply whether you are applying to government agencies, externships, or firms. But one tip on applying to be a prosecutor or public defender; you should be ready to perform a mock cross-examination or direct examination as at least some jurisdictions require that you do so in the interview. Regardless of where you interview, speaking with people at the firm, company, or government agency will give you a good lens into the interview process.

3. Dress to Impress

This may go without saying, but keep it cute and simple. Basically, you don't want your outfit to be a distraction, but there is no need to stifle creativity. Nothing will ruin confidence more than being uncomfortable in your interview suit. Ladies and fellas alike should dress professionally. The law is still a pretty formal profession. That stated, when interviewing, try to avoid bright colors and wear a suit that fits well (not too tight, not too loose). Basically, dress as you would if you were going to be in front of a judge. You may also want to avoid loud jewelry and strong fragrances. At the end of the day, you want to look nice, but you want your credentials and interviewing skills to be the thing that impresses them most—nothing else.

B. 2L2: Looking Toward the Summer

Once you have committed to a summer position, you want to do everything in your power to get a job offer. You should speak with former summer associates to learn what they did to convert their summer positions into full-time positions and speak with partners at the firm to learn what they are looking for in a summer associate. You should aim to submit exceptional work. In addition, try to meet as many people as you can within the organization and gain an understanding of the culture. Schedule lunch and coffees with attorneys within your organization. Take advantage of people's willingness to help you as you start your career.

If you didn't land a summer associate position, seek feedback from those who interviewed you. Try to schedule a coffee with some of your interviewers with whom you connected and seek feedback. When you get feedback, be willing to change and be grateful that they were candid (hopefully they will be candid). Furthermore, at the end of the follow-up meeting, you will want to ask your interviewers whether they have anyone they recommend you speak with about open summer positions. Additionally, ask your career advisor about firms that hire 3Ls. Network not just with attorneys but also with recruiting staff—they have more power than you think, trust me.

C. I Still Don't Have A Job

Now, if after applying through OCI you find that you still don't have a job, keep applying. There are hundreds of law firms; depending on where you live, there may be hundreds of firms in your city alone. There are also many nonprofit organizations, government agencies, and companies that need lawyers. If you do not have a job going into your third year, you should make a mass mailing plan. Or mass emailing, depending on how the firms you are targeting accept application materials. I personally think mailing a well-organized packet to a firm, even when they are not hiring, won't hurt. I actually did that for one large multinational firm and when they started hiring they invited me in for an interview and eventually gave me a job offer. You may be thinking, "But I don't have time!" To that I would say you likely have more time than you think, and if you are organized you can get this done. Try to mail a complete application packet to just ***one firms a day***. Or prepare one application packet a day, starting on Monday, and mail them off at the end of the week. The goal is to get your materials in front of as many potential employers as possible. Think about it: They are not going to come to you, so you must go to them. Then, after you've mailed your application packet to a firm, reach out to an attorney there—preferably one you know or one you can build camaraderie with quickly—and schedule a call or coffee. During the call or coffee, let the attorney know that you have sent in an application packet for the firm to keep on file in the event an opening arises. I recommend that you tell them you've applied in person because it may be off-putting to convey that information in an email and might even dissuade the attorney from agreeing to a meeting unless you already have an interview scheduled. Also, be sure to contact your alumni office and request a schedule of alumni events and ask for permission to attend; it's really important that you become an active participant in your alumni network. I mean, after all, you are paying for access to that network. Use it. Get your money's worth.

D. Extra-Curricular Activities

In addition to OCI, your second year will be spent getting involved with activities. Law review is the holy grail of student activities. A law review is a scholarly journal focusing on various legal issues that is published by an organization of students at a law school. At some schools, you will need to be invited to join the publication team at other schools you can participate in a writing competition against your peers to join the publication team. Check with your law school to learn the requirements for law review at your school. In addition to law review, many schools offer a wide-array of other publications that you can join. Typically, there are different positions that you can have as a member of a journal's publication team. Regardless of whether you join law review or another journal, you will likely benefit from editing scholarly articles and working with your peers to run a scholarly publication.

Joining a club in law school has many benefits and I highly recommend being involved if you can do so without sacrificing your grades. I participated on the Journal of International Law and Business at Northwestern and served on the mock trial team. I also served as a student leader for an international trip to Morocco, where we studied women's rights issues. The majority of the friendships I formed while in school came as a result of my involvement in student organizations. It is a phenomenal way to network with your peers and get to know your classmates.

"It's a slow process, but quitting won't speed it up"
—Unknown

CHAPTER IX.

IT'S NOT OVER TILL' IT'S OVER: 3L YEAR

During your third year of law school ("3L year"), you may feel as though you are just ready to practice—at least that's how I felt. But don't give up. Contrary to popular belief, there is still quite a bit of value in 3L year. I actually started working at the firm where I began my career during my third year of law school. I really enjoyed working at a large law firm during my third year because it gave me perspective. The 3L year is a great time to work as long as, by this time, you have a strong handle on your classes and other academic obligations.

Take classes that interest you during your 3L year. In addition to working, of course, I still had to maintain my grades, which was made easier by the fact that during my 3L year I took classes that I cared about. I took electives taught by brilliant adjunct professors on interesting and engaging subjects. I highly recommend this approach, especially if you have satisfied your requirements and your future employer has not mandated that you take additional doctrinal courses. I recommend you take classes that will teach you how to actually practice law—courses that teach you how to draft discovery responses or write defensive motions are very helpful. These classes often take the form of electives and can include practicums and clinics. Try to take classes that require you to draft motions, conduct arguments, or draft contracts. Those classes will help you develop the skills you will undoubtedly use in practice. Plus, to be honest, if you learn and apply yourself, they shouldn't be the classes that tank your GPA.

1. Confirm Your Graduation Requirements

During the first semester of your third year it is vital that you check and recheck your graduation requirements. You should become well-acquainted with your school's registrar so that you can easily confirm that you have taken all the electives and required courses necessary to graduate. In addition, if you are aiming for honors or another special designation, this is the office that can tell you those requirements. I was very intent on graduating with honors and, because I transferred from one law school to another, it was important that I learned the requirements to do so. Simply put, you are going into a profession with quite a few requirements. Know them and learn them.

2. Fulfill the Requirements to Practice Law

The requirements to practice law are rigorous. Earlier, I suggested that you apply for the character and fitness portion of the bar examination. In addition to the bar examination, which all of you have likely heard about, you also have to pass the Multistate Professional Responsibility Examination ("MPRE") to practice law. I recommend you sit for the MPRE during your second year of law school, but you can complete the exam in your third year as well. The MPRE is a two-hour, 60-question multiple-choice examination developed by the National Conference of Bar Examiners, which is the same organization that develops the tests given during the bar examination. The MPRE is administered three times per year and is required for admission to the bars of almost all United States jurisdictions. In addition to taking a course in legal ethics, I recommend using one of the many study aids that assists students in preparing for the MPRE. After all, it is an important test, and who doesn't want to know all of the laws surrounding acting ethically?

Though some people take this exam *after* sitting for the bar examination, I don't recommend that approach. You have to pass the MPRE before you can practice and be sworn in and I have known people who failed the MPRE on their first attempt but passed the bar examination. Avoid the unnecessary stress and take the MPRE early. To prepare for the MPRE, I took Themis Bar Review's online MPRE course, which allowed me to complete hundreds of multiple-choice questions before the actual examination, which helped tremendously.

a. Prepare for the Bar Examination

You can start passively preparing for the bar examination during your 3L year. Start reading blogs about bar examination preparation. If you love supplements, like I do, then start purchasing the supplements that you might want to use during bar preparation. Plan where you will study and which bar preparation course you will use.

All bar preparation courses are not created equal. Here's the thing: Most students learn differently. Therefore, while many bar preparation courses review the same content, the way each presents that content will differ. You need to select a bar preparation course that presents content in a way that you will best retain the information. I selected Themis and it worked wonderfully for me. I felt well prepared for the bar exam, and after I took the bar I felt as though I had passed. My closest friend from law school, however, used Barbri and also felt prepared for the exam. I had another friend that used Kaplan and also passed the bar exam. There is no magical bar preparation course that guarantees you will pass the exam, but the way the information is presented, the amount of homework given, and the level of personal interaction with the professors teaching the materials differs greatly.

Themis was 100 percent online. I liked that because law students can be negative, especially during bar preparation time, and I am not a negative person and try not to engage in negative conversations. What do I mean by that? Neither in law school nor while studying for the bar did I engage in conversations including statements such as "I will never pass this test" or "This is the worst exam of my life." I just don't find that kind of talk productive. But the only way I could completely control my environment, or so I thought, was by studying for the exam in the comfort of my own home. I determined who came in and out of my home and I didn't have to worry about being distracted while trying to study. That being said, I had a dedicated home office that made studying conducive. And I knew that I had enough determination to actually study without a professor standing in front of me requiring me to do so. But you have to be honest with yourself. I had a friend who used Themis, and she was not comfortable with the format and self-directed studying and didn't have the best experience with it, whereas I enjoyed studying for the bar examination online. Although studying for the bar may be the most important thing in your life after law school, I understand that for some people, financial responsibilities abound. That's why, before starting bar study, you should plan financially.

Plan financially before bar study begins so that when bar study starts you have a plan in place and all you need to do is work your plan. You have to know how your bills will get paid while you are studying for the bar. If you must work while studying for the bar, consider having an early conversation with your employer about the fact that you are taking the bar exam and will need time off from work to sit for the exam. Hopefully, you have an understanding employer, but if not, try to save up enough vacation early in the year to allow you to take at least the week of the bar exam off from work. Otherwise, get a calendar and plan every single minute of your day. Plan to wake up two hours earlier to start with bar study, use your lunch breaks to study for the bar, and the evenings will be dedicated almost exclusively to studying for the bar, along with most, if not all, Saturdays. Still, work in one day (mine was always Sunday) where you take a break and spend some time with family (hopefully family members who won't bring up the bar exam!). And remember, this is temporary. You are working toward a big goal, so it takes sacrifice, temporarily. Well, you will sacrifice a lot when practicing too, but let's deal with that when we have to. The first step is getting you admitted to the bar.

Having an employer that covers bar expenses is great, but you should be clear on what, exactly, your employer will cover. If your employer is covering bar expenses, which many large law firms do, then you should review the policy on what the employer will cover versus what you will need to pay for yourself. Some employers cover

MPRE expenses, bar examination expenses, attorney registration fees, bar preparation course expenses and provide a stipend. If you are blessed enough to have multiple job opportunities out of law school, you should ask which bar expenses the employer covers, if any. Be sure to inquire into the amount of the stipend (this information is often available online). Also, when researching what your employer will cover, find out if you can directly bill the firm for bar expenses or whether the firm will reimburse you for expenses paid out of pocket. This will help you plan how much money is required up front to cover your expenses.

If you do not have an employer that will cover expenses, you don't have a job to help with expenses, and your family does not support you financially, there are still options that can help you lift the heavy burden of bar expenses: (1) bar scholarships and (2) bar loans. You can search for both via a simple Google search. It wouldn't be wise for me to provide a list, since many of those resources change over time, but ask your school for help in finding both, as they will undoubtedly have resources that you can use. Bottom line, if you don't need to work while studying for the bar, don't; but if you do, you can still pass the bar exam—it just takes some planning.

Another significant consideration when studying for the bar exam is how to maintain relationships that matter to you while studying. Talk to your friends and family about bar preparation in terms that will illustrate the magnitude of the journey that you are preparing to embark upon. I frequently told friends and family, "Look, I am about to study for the bar exam so I may miss some functions and activities because I have to focus on passing this exam. If I don't, the past three years will have gone to waste. I literally cannot practice law without passing this test." That being said, it is also important to maintain the relationships that you've developed, especially for those students who are married or who have children. It's okay to take a break, spend time with friends, or go on a date night with your significant other. If you regularly attend church, keep going. For me, maintaining some consistency and partaking in activities that I enjoyed helped me keep perspective. The bar is important, but it is not life or death. Give it the time and respect that it deserves, but there are twenty-four hours in a day, and taking two of them for yourself will not cause you to fail the bar exam. Pace yourself, breathe, and succeed.

"Never say never, because limits, like fears, are often just an illusion."
—Michael Jordan

CHAPTER X.

You control your destiny: Transferring law schools

We have talked a lot about the things that can help to propel your legal career, with the first being good grades and the second being attending a highly ranked law school. But what if you don't receive admission into a highly ranked law school the first time around; do you have any options? Yes, you may have the option—after your first year of law school—to transfer to a more highly ranked law school. Why would you transfer law schools? People decide to transfer law schools for all types of reasons, with the most common being that attending a highly ranked law school increases your job prospects, which is why I transferred. I wanted to attend a T-14 law school to increase my chances of receiving a job offer from a large law firm. For me, that worked. Your best—best, not only—chance of landing a prestigious summer associate position that may lead to a full-time six-figure job offer upon graduation is to obtain excellent grades at a top law school.

A. How to Transfer

If you would like to transfer law schools, you must begin by mapping out your plan during your first year of law school. You can start applying to transfer as early as the spring semester of your 1L year. Focus on getting great grades at your current law school. I mean really outstanding grades. Unlike when you first apply to law school, when you transfer, your LSAT and undergraduate GPA is not the most important factor in whether or not you will gain admittance into a top-ranked law school. The most important factor for most top schools is your 1L law school grades. That being said, don't inundate your résumé with clubs and activities that will prevent you from getting outstanding grades in your 1L courses—remember, grades matter most. That's a recurring theme.

In addition to getting good grades, you should start developing relationships with your professors because you will need letters of recommendation. You will eventually need to ask your current law school's professors to recommend you to attend another law school—weird, right? But you are likely not the first student to make such a request. Some professors may flat-out refuse. I had great relationships with all of my first-year professors, but one of my favorite professors refused, as he had a firm policy against writing letters of recommendation to help students transfer to other law schools. No worries—you have various professors you should be able to ask. To be safe, I asked five professors to write me letters of recommendation. I only needed three, but I wanted to ensure that even if two turned in their letters late or refused, I had enough letters to complete my application. Also, make sure the letters are positive. That should go without saying.

You should also be prepared to submit a writing sample and a personal statement. The writing sample part is easy, as you can use one of your writing assignments from your legal writing course, but the personal statement is often more daunting. Your personal statement needs to answer two questions, whether explicitly asked by the school or not: (1) why you want to attend that school *specifically* and (2) why you will be a successful alumnus of the law school to which you are applying. Remember, when you transfer, you are joining a new community, and the school likely wants to know how you will contribute to that community while a student and beyond.

Learn about the schools to which you are applying as a transfer student by talking to alumni, current students, and professors. You should also visit the school and attend a class if you can. Then, in your personal statement, write about how your conversations with alumni and the classes you attended solidified your interest in the school. It may not be feasible to do this for 10 law schools, but if you have a first choice, maybe this is the route you take for your dream law school. I took my own advice, and before applying to Northwestern as a transfer student, I spoke to students, alumni, and professors and wrote about it in my personal statement. I have wanted to attend Northwestern since completing a high school debate summer camp on Northwestern's undergraduate campus. Therefore, I went above and beyond in my application. It was essential that I be admitted. Do you need to do all these things to get admitted? No, but I am of the mind that you do all that you can so that no matter the result, you know you tried your best.

When transferring, it is important to keep a calendar of application due dates for all schools to which you are applying. Some schools allow you to apply early—before spring semester grades are released—and others do not. Moreover, some schools offer transfer students scholarships and others do not. This is important because law school is very expensive and it makes sense to at least apply to some of the schools that offer transfer students scholarships—call around to find out which schools offer scholarships.Many do not, but this is not a hard and fast rule for all schools.

B. Was It Worth It?

Because of the high cost of transferring law schools—as many do not offer scholarships—I am frequently asked whether I recommend transferring schools. To that question, I always answer in the affirmative. For me, transferring was a great decision. I was able to increase my earning potential substantially and attended the institution of my dreams. As cheesy as that sounds, it's true! I had a great experience at Northwestern.

I've talked about the positives of transferring, but there are some downsides. First, as discussed, transfer students often do not receive scholarships. I did not receive any scholarship money from Northwestern—this was by far the biggest downside. Other than that, I had to leave the strong bonds that I had made with my 1L friends, but I was lucky in that my two closest friends from law school also transferred, so we stayed in touch and still remain very close. My new classmates were professional and building new relationships was not difficult, but that, of course, will vary from person to person. Here's the thing: I transferred because it had the potential to help my career, and it did. You will need to weigh the pros and cons for yourself, but don't let fear be the reason you don't make the jump—or at minimum apply.

Now, if you decide to transfer, make sure you can still participate in on-campus interviewing and law review or another scholarly journal. You will also want to inquire about mock trial and moot court opportunities if you are concerned about participating in those activities. I joined a journal and mock trial at my new school and I thought it was a good experience, but you need to make sure these experiences do not affect your ability to perform well. When you transfer, you will need to re-establish your

GPA, meaning you are starting over academically. So that first semester at your new school is extremely important. Look up the requirements to graduate with honors early on, try to find a 3L mentor who has performed well at your new school, and keep your eye on the prize.

Is transferring the right decision for everyone? No. You have to figure out whether it's the best decision for you, but here's a pro tip: you can apply to transfer law schools even if you don't want to transfer. Then, you might be able to use the fact that you have received admittance into a higher ranked school to negotiate additional scholarship money at your current law school—so whether you leave or not, I don't see any negatives in applying. There is some power in having options.

Deciding to attend law school is a huge investment of time, money, and energy, so if you're going to do it, do it right! Put in the work to get the grades,complete internships,and transfer schools if you feel it will help your legal career. A law degree is expensive, so make sure that when you look at that piece of paper, you don't regret your decision. Hopefully this book has provided you with the tools you need to conquer the law school hustle!

APPENDIX A

HELPFUL LAW SCHOOL SUPPLEMENTS[16]

NAME OF SUPPLEMENT	COST	DESCRIPTION
Glannon Guides	$20.00 - $37.00	Glannon Guides are exceptional supplements on a wide-range of legal topics, but I personally recommend *the Glannon Guide to Civil Procedure: Learning Civil Procedure Through Multiple-Choice Questions and Analysis*. These guides are particularly useful for multiple choice examinations.

---

[16] All of these supplements can be found on Amazon, and the prices vary depending on whether you purchase the supplements used or new. The prices contained here are mere estimates for new copies of the supplements. Be wary of purchasing supplements that are too old because laws change and you do not want to learn old law. Although all of the supplements listed cost money, sometimes the student representatives for the large bar examination preparation course providers, such as Barbri, Kaplan and Themis, offer free supplements to 1L law students. Be sure to ask your school's representatives about such supplements.

NAME OF SUPPLEMENT	COST	DESCRIPTION
Examples and Explanations	$30.00 - $50.00	The Examples and Explanations (E&E) supplement is great, particularly for essay exams. While in law school I used E&E guides to study for property, contracts, and constitutional law.
Law in a Flash	$30.00 - $100.00	Law in a Flash flashcards are great to assist with memorizing black letter law and practicing your knowledge of the law through hypotheticals. I recommend these flashcards for contracts, civil procedure, constitutional law, legal ethics and evidence.

NAME OF SUPPLEMENT	COST	DESCRIPTION
Quimbee	$15.00 - $24.00/month	Quimbee is an online subscription that provides cases already briefed (among other things) in the IRAC format by attorneys. I found these pre-made case briefs to be exceptional. I highly recommend using this service.

CPSIA information can be obtained
at www.ICGtesting.com
Printed in the USA
LVHW01s0444090918
589486LV00007B/63/P